Captain Jack Malloch
The Life and Times of a Rhodesian Entrepreneur

A sad tale from Africa

By
Dan Remenyi

First edition, 2014

Copyright© 2014 the Author

All rights reserved. No part of this publication may be reproduced in any material form (including photocopying or storing in any medium by electronic means and whether or not transiently or incidentally to some other use of this publication) without the written permission of the copyright holder except in accordance with the provisions of the Copyright Designs and Patents Act 1988, or under the terms of a licence issued by the Copyright Licensing Agency Ltd, Saffron House, 6-10 Kirby Street, London EC1N 8TS. Applications for the copyright holder's written permission to reproduce any part of this publication should be addressed to the publishers.

Disclaimer: While every effort has been made by the editor, authors and the publishers to ensure that all the material in this book is accurate and correct at the time of going to press, any error made by readers as a result of any of the material, formulae or other information in this book is the sole responsibility of the reader. Readers should be aware that the URLs quoted in the book may change or be damaged by malware between the time of publishing and accessing by readers.

Paperback book ISBN: 978-1-910309-15-5
Hardback book ISBN: 978-1-910309-21-6
e-Pub ISBN: 978-1-910309-14-8
Kindle ISBN: 978-1-910309-17-9

Published by: ACPIL, Reading, RG4 9SJ, United Kingdom,
info@academic-publishing.org

Available from www.academic-bookshop.com

Cover photos

Jack Malloch photograph supplied by Mrs Blythe Kruger from the family's private collection.

Affretair DC-8:
http://commons.wikimedia.org/wiki/File:Affretair_Douglas_DC-8_Marmet-3.jpg

Rhodesian Coat of Arms:
http://upload.wikimedia.org/wikipedia/commons/4/40/Rhodesian_coat_of_arms_Sag.svg

About the author

Dan Remenyi moved to Rhodesia from South Africa in 1965, just in time to witness Ian Smith declare Southern Rhodesia independent from Great Britain and set up what was to become the Republic of Rhodesia. He met Jack Malloch in December 1966 and worked for him (or more correctly for Air Trans Africa) on and off over the next few years while he finished his university degree in economics and political science. On completion of his degree Dan worked for Air Trans Africa for two years before returning to South Africa in 1970 to continue his studies. He retained occasional contact with Jack and other members of Air Trans Africa over the following decade.

Dan Remenyi who now lives in Oxfordshire has worked as a researcher and lecturer in business and management at various universities in Europe and Africa over the past 25 years. He has written numerous books on research practice. He has written one other biographic monograph called the Story of Steve which is set in Ireland, South Africa and Rhodesia.

Another history book by the same author:

The Story of Steve – An Immigrant's Tale
e-Pub ISBN 978-1-910309-16-2
Paper ISBN 978-1-905305-66-4

Contents

Preface	i
Prologue	iii
Acknowledgements	v
Dedication	vi
Where to begin the story?	1
The Air Trans Africa family	18
The challenge for airlines and airline entrepreneurs	30
Africa evolves	34
The winds of change	36
Back in Africa	44
Jack and Nigeria	54
The emergence of Biafra	57
A Rhodesian entrepreneur	60
What happens in war!	65
Back in Salisbury	73
The building of Affretair	78
Kissinger pulls the plug?	88
Jack and the chilled beef	92
Decorations and Honors	96
And the Spitfire	98
And the Fat Lady Sang	103
A sad tale from Africa	104
Looking back from the 21st century	106
Index	112

Jack Malloch – Rhodesian Extraordinaire

Preface

On a number of occasions I sat in the dreary Air Trans Africa offices at Salisbury Airport with Bob and Iris Nesbit wondering if the company could survive the next few months. We basically thought that it could and we really hoped that it would. But there was not much evidence to support our feelings. This little company went through a number of very difficult periods when it came within a hair's breadth of having to be closed due to financial difficulties.

Bob and I said to ourselves a number of times, "We should write a book about Air Trans Africa" but Iris would say, "Who do you think would believe you? What happens around here is so improbable. This place is the epitome of the aphorism that Truth is Stranger than Fiction."

Well, the years went by and nothing was written. It is now nearly 50 years ago that this story started and of course my memory is not what it used to be. And furthermore a number of the people I would now like to consult about the details of what happened have passed away.

I was spurred on to write this by a few odd comments I heard and read describing Jack as a gunrunner and a freebooter which I feel are misinformed and unfair descriptions of him. I have also read that Jack made himself very rich out of sanction busting with the implication that he was somehow profiteering from this situation. This I do not believe either. I have no illusions that Jack was popular with everyone; I am aware that he had detractors and I do know of his shortcomings.

In writing this I realised that the story only makes sense when it is understood in the context of the Rhodesian Unilateral Declaration of Independence, the collapse of the Portuguese in Africa and the ensuing Bush War and these issues have had to be addressed.

It is also important in this story that the Nigerian Civil War be addressed as it was an important aspect of Jack's life.

I know that parts of this story have been told elsewhere and that the detail of the events will not perfectly match other sources as there is misinformation about Jack on the web. I have tried to be as accurate and as frank as I can be.

Dan Remenyi
dan.remenyi@gmail.com
May 2014

Prologue

This book started out as an account of some of the main events experienced by Air Trans Africa and its owner Captain Jack Malloch. However, as I described these events I came to realise that the Jack Malloch story had to be told in the context of what was happening in Southern Africa and also in relation to some of the events in Nigeria at that time.

As I was writing this account I realised that much of what I have said could be explored in much greater detail if I had a few years to write this book. I freely admit that some of my account will be regarded by some as being a high level overview. It is also inevitable that some readers will find my narrative incomplete. However I have not written this book for expert historians but rather for those who want an overview of the situation and the circumstances faced by Jack and Air Trans Africa.

I have tried not to be judgemental but I do know that many of the issues and the incidents which I mention are sensitive and there will be those who strongly disagree with the way I have presented some of the issues. It is not my intention to offend anyone although it is probably not possible to avoid so doing.

I am not entirely a pacifist but I believe that war should only be engaged in as a very last resort primarily because of the enormous hardship it brings to so many people, even to those who have no direct part in it.

I found this book much more difficult to research and write than I had imagined. Jack Malloch was a secretive man and because of the wars being fought during this period there is not much information in the public domain. Furthermore the information which is available is often contradictory. I think that this is the nature of a story such as this.

I also need to say that as I finished this book I became quite sad about the events described herein. Jack's was not an easy life and the events surrounding his life and times were highly destructive for many people's lives and opportunities. The Romans had a saying which translates into something similar to "Out of Africa there is always something new". In modern times perhaps the saying might be changed to "Out of Africa there is always something sad".

Acknowledgements

I would like to acknowledge the ORAFS (Old Rhodesian Air Force So-and-sos) blog administered by Eddy Norris. Through this blog I was put in touch with a number of helpful people.

I would like to thank Blythe Kruger who is Jack Malloch's sister for her kind help. It has been a pleasure and an honour to speak with this charming lady about her memories from this period.

I am very grateful for the photographic images I have been supplied with by a number of old Rhodesians and wherever possible I have acknowledged the sources of these in the book.

Dedication

In the first instance this book is dedicated to the memory of Captain Jack Malloch who was no doubt an extraordinary leader. He was a man driven by his love for aviation and his need to be an independent entrepreneur. He was neither a freebooter nor a gun runner. He did not enrich himself from profiteering at the expense of his country during its very difficult predicament. On his death he left behind many friends who greatly admired him.

I would also like to dedicate this book to the memory of Bob and Iris Nesbit who were good, loyal and thoroughly effective foot soldiers in "Malloch's Air Force".

Jack Malloch – Rhodesian Extraordinaire

In the early 1950s emigration to Southern Rhodesia was promoted in Great Britain with the slogan that it was the land of Sunshine and Opportunity. It was proudly declared to be a beautiful country with one of the best climates in the world. It was a land where the good life could be had. Yet within just over a decade this country began to slide into a civil war in which more than 20,000 people lost their lives and from which the country has not yet recovered. Although born in South Africa John McVicar Malloch, known to all as Jack Malloch, chose to live and work in this country where he excelled as an aviator and an entrepreneur. As an aviator he brought larger and longer range aircraft to the country and as an entrepreneur he developed an international business across countries in both Africa and Europe.

Where to begin the story?

Jack shortly before flying his Spitfire.

Jack Malloch was happy in the cockpit as it took him away from everyday life down on the earth below. The African landscape can be very attractive from the air, especially if you are not flying at too high an altitude. He was one of those men who had taken to flying right from the very beginning and he needed no encouragement whatsoever to be winging above us all. He had after all effectively grown up in the air as a result of being accepted into the Southern Rhodesian Auxiliary Air Force[1] as a young man and then flying off to war in Europe as a fighter pilot. As a young fighter pilot he had been shot down behind enemy lines and had to lie low with the partisans in Italy until they were able to get him out. Coming back to the slow pace of life in Southern Rhodesia after the war did not offer much excitement to this young man.

Perhaps Jack's main problem was that he was also one of those men who didn't want a boss and that meant he had to work for himself rather than be a stick jockey in someone else's airline - to be the master of his own destiny and not just another pilot flying routine short hops around the Rhodesias and Nyasaland was very important to him. This meant that he needed to have his own airline and this presented a significant problem for a man with limited resources who was living in the small landlocked country of Rhodesia in the 1960s. Less ambitious men might have settled for a small number of little aircraft flying around the region and it is true to say that Captain Jack started that way with an airline which was called Fish Air. This little operation flew up and down to the coast landing at exotic destinations such as Beira, Vilanculos and Inhassoro and did exactly what its name implies, carry fish. But this did not satisfy Jack and he moved on to bigger issues and bigger airplanes. After being involved for a while with Rhodesian Air Services at Salisbury Airport which primarily operated a small network of scheduled services within Rhodesia, Jack began his own airline in 1965 aimed at providing intercontinental air transport, which he called Air Trans Africa or ATA for short. He was a man who liked to do things that hadn't been

---

[1] Over the period of this story the Air Force in Rhodesia changed its name a number of times.

done before. He wanted to fly to places and in aircraft that other Rhodesians hadn't. In the eyes of some people in Salisbury this meant that Jack was prepared to go where angels fear to tread and this caused discomfort and suspicion of him in some circles.

His vision of how a long range airline would benefit his country was certainly ahead of its time. ATA was a grand name which articulated this vision of flying long distance. Nearly everybody associated with ATA was very proud of this name and although in the mid-1960s Jack had a long way to go to make his airline into an international operator, most people associated with Air Trans Africa felt that he was the man who could succeed at this.

Salisbury Airport with Air Rhodesia's Viscounts and DC-3s. Jack's larger aircraft are not at this point visible.
Source: Paul Dubois from private collection.

This belief in Jack Malloch was entirely based on his charismatic leadership. There was virtually no reason to believe that the fledgling Air Trans Africa would not crash and burn financially, to use an aviation metaphor. But Jack had unusual charisma, and this was despite the fact he was a medium height, slightly overweight, bald man who could not by any stretch of the imagination be regarded as a striking or handsome figure. Neither did Jack dress especially well. If anything he mostly looked ever so slightly untidy and often presented himself as being somewhat stressed by the many issues which no doubt challenged him every day. In those days he regularly patted or rubbed his bald head while he thought about what to say or do next.

An important aspect of Jack's leadership skills was his ability to make the people with whom he was working feel that they were really important to the task in hand. He was especially skilled in this respect and this generated in certain people a high degree of loyalty to him personally.

But despite this Jack clearly stood out in a crowd. There was a definite inner confidence which he exuded. He always spoke quietly and nearly always in a reassuring tone. He was a person who gave the impression that what you had to say was of some importance to him and when appropriate, he smiled generously. Many years later it became fashionable in management theory circles to talk about the non-heroic leader, i.e. the leader who does not go in for the razzmatazz of being out in front of the pack, and Jack was indeed a good example of such a leader.

Jack photographed during the early days of ATA.
Source: Private collection of Greg Malloch

It is also worth pointing out that Jack was reputed, at least by some of the Air Trans Africa staff, to know everyone of importance in Rhodesia and further afield. Jack had flown in the same fighter squadron as the Prime Minister Ian Smith, and it was assumed by the people around him that he had access to people at the highest level. In fact there was very little evidence of this, especially in the early days of Air Trans Africa, but the story made some of the people who worked for Jack think that they were rubbing shoulders with a very important person, and indeed in some sense they were. But Jack was never part of the inner circle of the transport policy establishment in Rhodesia. And this was a man who before joining the RRAF had been a lorry driver for the Southern Rhodesia Railways. What a remarkable transformation, one wonders! Jack Malloch was a need-to-know man and therefore he spoke very little about his connection in government and elsewhere. He was also slow to reveal the business issues that were pressing on his mind. But everyone at Air Trans Africa knew that Jack was the man who was going to end up with the most important airline in Rhodesia.

So let me start this story when I first got involved with Air Trans Africa at a time when it looked like the company was going to be in some really very serious financial trouble.

I met Jack Malloch because I was sent out to the Air Trans Africa offices at Salisbury Airport by the company's auditors on a final rescue mission. The senior partner in the audit practice located in the centre of the town had recruited me for a special short term project and told me that Air Trans Africa was about to be closed down by the Tax Collectors as there appeared to be a big tax bill outstanding. The Rhodesian Receiver of Revenue was known to be efficient and thorough and they wanted what they believed, and estimated, to be due to them. After all the company had visible assets in the form of large and apparently expensive airplanes which were parked on the taxi way at Salisbury airport.

The company had 60 days before the bailiffs would be sent in, the assets confiscated and a lock put on the door. The company was showing a huge profit in the last version of the draft financial accounts, but there was hardly a penny in the bank. I cannot recall how much money the tax people believed they were owed by Air Trans Africa, but it was a very large sum and Air Trans Africa was truly flat broke. There was no question of an overdraft from the bank of any sort or size. The company was so short of money that the staff were not able to be paid their salaries and this had been the case for a number of months. The auditors and I speculated a bit as to how these circumstances had come about. The senior partner said, "There is no doubt that the financial systems in Air Trans Africa leave quite a lot to be desired but my distinct impression is that all the people there who handle any of the money that goes through the business are really quite honest. We are not looking for fraud; we are looking for incomplete record keeping. There was an accountant there but he has gone. I think he had a drinking problem. He left abruptly and there was no hand over. No one knows where he is and he probably wouldn't talk to us anyway. We put together a draft set of accounts using the unchecked numbers from the ledgers and they showed a remarkably big profit. The reality is that there is no one left out there now in the business who knows a debt from a credit. Everyone is going to be helpful to you because they know how much trouble they will be in if we can't sort out the apparent tax debt. You have only to worry about the draft accounts which run up to about 15 months ago and you need to sort them out urgently. Forget about the current accounting and financial problems of which there are plenty. We can think about these and sort them out later when this tax crisis is over".

I had applied to a somewhat vague advertisement for a temporary post as a bookkeeper/accountant and I had expected to be stuck in some little office doing routine ledger work. I was quite literally flabbergasted at the prospect of such an interesting sounding job. "Do you think that you are capable of doing this work for us?" the senior partner asked me. "Of course", I replied crossing my figures beneath the desk. "This should not be all that big a problem", I said, hoping to convince myself. After all I had written up the books of accounts for an electrical repair business, a grocery shop, a language school and several farmers. I had been told that if you can write up a set of accounts for a farmer you know all there is to know about accounting.

But I was very glad that no dishonesty was suspected as I was not in any sense qualified to perform any forensic auditing or accounting and, much more importantly, I did not want to be in a position where I was trying to catch people's misdemeanours.

The reason I was employed was that the auditors did not want to spend their own time working on the accounts of this small company as they were of the view that they might not get paid. There was also the question of whether the auditors should be writing up the books for their clients anyway. In fact my appointment was the last ditch attempt by the senior partner to avoid the embarrassment of being the auditor of a reasonably visible company which was likely to experience the public humiliation of bankruptcy and sequestration. I was therefore recruited for a special project at what was for me a reasonable salary, but nothing like the fee that the audit partners would have been looking for. I was sent out to Salisbury airport with the commission to either confirm Air Trans Africa's tax debt or to find a way out of it by the end of the month.

"By the way", said the senior audit partner, "Air Trans Africa is a rather strange place. It is quite odd. It is unlike any other place I have audited before. It is rather eerie in some ways. It had a lot of bad publicity some months back when they had a series of aircraft break down in Europe and hundreds of holidaymakers were stranded. I don't know if they will ever recover from that. I will pick you up tomorrow and take you out there and then you will be on your own. Remember this is a time critical situation".

Previous to this job I had worked in accounting for Air Rhodesia and I had often looked across into the Air Trans Africa hanger at the bigger planes which were parked there. Air Rhodesia had a small fleet of Vickers Viscounts, whereas Jack's airline had considerably bigger aircraft. People who worked at Salisbury airport knew virtually nothing about Jack and Air Trans Africa. It was a secretive sort of place and there was a general feeling of suspicion about this man who had all these airplanes and was said to own them privately. Other than the sometimes troublesome passenger trips to Europe, where did Jack's airplanes fly and what did they carry? However this was not on my mind when I arrived in the offices adjacent to the Air Trans Africa hanger in December 1966. This was one of the biggest hangers at the airport which accommodated the wing span of a Lockheed Super Constellation (Super Connie) or a McDonald Douglas DC-7C.

Jack's Super Connie eventually became a club house as pictured above. The Super Connie was a luxurious aircraft in its day and popular with passengers.

Source: Undetermined.

Air Trans Africa had a large car park in front of the hangar in which 50 or maybe even 100 cars could be parked. In the years during which I was involved with Air Trans Africa I hardly ever saw more than 10 cars there and this no doubt contributed to other people working at the airport feeling that there was something weird going on at the company.

Air Trans Africa's offices were basically a lean-to shed-type building which adjoined the hanger and was made of breeze blocks. It was a strip of six fairly miserable offices. I guess that they were only just acceptable as a working place with old furniture and even older threadbare carpets, but then much of Air Trans Africa was of the same ilk. The premises were the sort that could be relied on to be very hot in summer and cold in winter. There were glass doors in front of the row of offices with a reception desk, although there was hardly ever anyone at the reception and indeed there was no receptionist. Jack's office was slightly better than the others in that it was at the far end of the row of six and it had two windows which made it a lot brighter and somewhat warmer than the others. The auditors explained my brief to Jack and two people working for him as administrators. This didn't take long as everyone knew that Air Trans Africa was in a serious position with the tax authorities. I was assured by Jack and his colleagues that any and all the documents relevant to the operation of the airline would be made available to me. Having been brought into the business by the auditors I was in a quite privileged position and everyone seemed to know that the work I was going to do over the next few weeks was going to be central to the survival of Air Trans Africa.

I was found a small desk in the corner of the office next to Jack's and without any further formalities I started by scrutinising the draft accounts and trying to find the audit trail which led from there. A mountain of lever arch files would later be produced along with what seemed to be endless correspondence between Air Trans Africa and other airlines and suppliers.

It is important to say that although Jack Malloch was without doubt a superb pilot and a great leader, he had in those days no sense at all for the attention to administrative detail necessary to run an organisation. Jack was in a number of ways an administrative disaster zone. This was brought about by a combination of his need-to-know mentality and the lack of paperwork which regularly failed to accompany the deals he made in various parts of the world. Also in those early days he was badly let down by some of the people he thought were looking after the official administration for him. Up to that point Jack had not been a good judge of accountants or administrators.

So, sitting at my little desk, I called for all the papers related to the cost of operating the company. Engineering and fuel consumption were among the first matters I was interested in. A veritable mountain of paper was produced which showed the cost of operating the engineering facility at Salisbury airport. I should immediately say that the paperwork of the organisation which did not pass through Jack's own hands was pretty complete, at least up to the date to which I was working. There were two administrative employees in the Air Trans Africa office - a married couple called Bob and Iris Nesbit who were sticklers for putting pieces of paper into the right files in the belief that someday someone would take them seriously. There were all sorts of costs associated with repairs to the aircraft while they were in the hanger at Salisbury airport, as well as when they were flying abroad, and the sums of money were really quite substantial.

I examined the audit trail carefully and came to the conclusion that the engineering costs were probably correct. When it came to fuel costs the situation was far more complicated. In those days captains were given a large sum of money in cash or traveller's cheques as a float when they departed on a long haul flight overseas. It was from this float that they purchased their fuel as well as paid all the other costs of the flight, including the crew expenses. In reality this could mean that a captain often took many thousands of pounds with him. Balancing all of this and making sure that everything was accounted for was quite a task. Despite this after some time I came to the conclusion that I was not going to find any serious error made in the recording of the financial aspects of the business.

I was now a couple of weeks into the job and I was not sure if I was going to succeed at my given objective. As a matter of pure routine I asked to see the registration papers for the aircraft and the certificates of ownership. "We don't own these aircraft, none of them", I was told. "Who does then?" I asked. In response I was told, "They are owned by a UK company from which Jack leases them directly. They are at one of the big airports in the UK near Luton, I think." "So what do they cost and how are they paid for?" I asked. "We don't really know," came the reply. "Jack has his own filing cabinet where he keeps documents to do with issues like that." And then without the slightest indication that this might have been unusual in any way, I was told, "I think that Jack pays for all the lease charges on the aircraft himself." "Well how does he do that?" I asked. Once again the reply could not have been anticipated, "I think that these things must be paid for directly out of Jack's personal Swiss Bank account".

What a surprising turn of events! So I took a long moment for reflection. Jack had a personal Swiss Bank account and furthermore Jack paid company expenses out of that account. Could this be right? Was this legal? There was a lot of exchange control around in those days. I had never met anyone with a Swiss Bank account before. Was it one of these special numbered accounts? No wonder the financial statements which were presented in Salisbury were incomplete. What was really interesting was that there was no real attempt to hide the fact that there was a parallel financial system running. All I had to do was to discover the right questions to ask. As far as the employees of Air Trans Africa were concerned, it was absolutely natural that Jack Malloch would be paying for things out of his own pocket without these transactions having to be recorded in the company's books of account. This was a symptom of a really important problem that Jack had with his business, which was his difficulty in keeping his own personal identity separate from the identity of the company. He never really achieved this.

All the work I had just done was in fact unnecessary. I could have solved the problem by asking one simple question of Jack Malloch, "Please show me your private files and the statements for your Swiss Bank account". Of course he would never have shown these to me just like that, but he could have listed all the payments he had made on items related to the operating of the aircraft while abroad.

It now only took a few days to solve the accounting and tax problems. I obtained a list of amounts of money directly expended by Jack Malloch for the business and this completely reversed the situation on the tax calculation. There was now a substantial established loss. Air Trans Africa was not after all going to be closed down by the taxman. I redrafted the accounts and presented them to the auditors. Great celebrations were had by everyone concerned. However the auditors were now of the view that they had completed everything they wanted to do for Air Trans Africa and they wanted to distance themselves from the company in case it had to be placed in receivership. For certain the company was still broke and it was not clear how it would be saved. The auditors agreed to pay me for another month so that I could steer the accounts through the taxman. I was then offered the opportunity of being employed directly by Air Trans Africa to set up some systems in the office that would prevent this sort of crisis from happening again.

I was delighted to take on this challenge as I had always had a special interest in aviation and even the small amount of contact I'd had with Jack Malloch up to that point made it clear to me that he was a man worth knowing and working for. I was also the only person around who knew the difference between a debit and a credit; at least, I knew the difference on a good day.

But before I get into some of the detail of Air Trans Africa there is a short side story to be told about the aviation industry in that part of the world at the time. Although the auditors were finishing off their work with Air Trans Africa they had another airline client called Bechuanaland National Airways located in the adjacent country of Botswana. The financial records of this airline were in more or less the same situation as Air Trans Africa. The books of account did not appear to correspond with what was going on and I was asked if I could go up to Francistown for just one day and have a look at the situation. It transpired that Jack needed to go there at about the same time and it was decided that he would fly himself in his executive plane, a de Havilland Dove, and I could accompany him. This was routine for Jack who made flying look absolutely natural, but it was a great new and exciting experience for me. I had only ever flown twice before in a South African Airways Vickers Viscount and on Air Rhodesia in a similar aircraft. It was good to be flying with someone so comfortable in the cockpit.

A de Havilland Dove similar to the one used by Air Trans Africa.

Source: http://commons.wikimedia.org/wiki/File:De_Havilland_Dove_D-INKA_(5932936601).jpg

Francistown was then a truly desolate little place especially for a day tripper with accounting problems on his mind. The airline's accounting problems were even more complicated than anticipated and they were in the end handed over to another firm who were pleased to spend time in Botswana sorting them out. However, in the mid-afternoon while I was finishing off my notes to this effect, Jack came into the office I was working in and said, "We have to leave immediately. Grab your papers and let's go." I had no idea what this was about but of course I instantly obliged. As we left the building and walked over to the aircraft I saw one huge black cloud rushing up from the horizon. "That black cloud is going to close this airport in 15 minutes," said Jack. "If we don't get out now we will be stuck here for the night". This was typical of the man of action which was Jack. The trip home was bumpy indeed and thus more than a little uncomfortable, but we arrived safely as expected. I used to wonder if Jack had bothered to tell air traffic control that he was taking off, but now I wonder if there even was an air traffic controller in Francistown in those days. This casual approach to flying and **the big black cloud** was to raise its head again later, actually at the very end of the story.

There is one other tale to tell which throws light on Air Trans Africa and Africa at that time. Jack had a considerable number of envelopes in his desk from the Malawi Government related to the company he had floated there some years ago. Jack had registered a company there called Malawi Air Freighters which he intended to use one day. However nothing had been done with regard to annual returns which were required by law and he had begun to receive letters threatening fines and penalties from the Companies Office in Blantyre. So I was asked if I would go to Blantyre and sort all this out. I was informed that Jack had an agent there to whom I should pay a visit and I was also asked to see the lawyer who had set up the company.

It was a short flight from Salisbury to Blantyre. The tiny airport at Blantyre was unremarkable except for the large sign which announced that long hair on men and short skirts on women were forbidden in Malawi. President Hastings Banda was somewhat out of date in his attitude towards 1960s fashions. I was met by a driver who told me that we had to rush into town because President Banda was expected to be using the road to the airport and when he was on a particular road no other traffic was allowed. I was accommodated in the Mount Soche Hotel which was certainly the best hotel I had stayed in up to that point.

The meetings with the Malawi Registrar of Companies and the lawyer went very well and all my objectives were achieved. However when I arrived at Air Trans Africa's agent's office the senior man had decided that I should, as Jack's representative, be introduced to several people in Government Departments. He also told me that he had been in touch with the Minister of Transport's office and that the Minister himself would be pleased to meet me. All this seemed to me to be positive and I had no problem in telling them what a interesting outfit Air Trans Africa was and how one day there might be an operation in Malawi, with their approval of course.

The difficulty was that these meetings took more time than originally estimated and I ended up with a mad dash to the airport and despite the fact that I was only a few minutes late and the passengers had not yet boarded the airplane, the ground staff had closed the flight and they refused to take me.

Blantyre Airport was tiny and it was clear to everyone around me what my circumstances were. While in this state of shock as I had not ever missed a flight before, I was tapped on the shoulder by a man whom I had never seen before and who said, "I have my own airplane, single engine Cessna, and I will be flying myself to Salisbury in about 30 minutes. If you and your luggage are not too heavy I will be pleased to take you home".

I was so delighted at this invitation. What a wonderfully nice man this was. But then I was directed to the weighting platform and together with my luggage I came to 10 kilos more that the prescribed takeoff weight for that aircraft at that airport under the conditions of that day.

So I spent another night at the Mount Soche Hotel.

When I returned to Air Trans Africa the following day I was surprised to be told that I was very lucky that I had not flown with this unknown man. I was told that anyone who would not fly because of being so little over weight did not know what they were doing as a pilot. I was told how Jack and others had flown aircraft which were well above their technically legal limit with no adverse effect whatsoever. I have always wondered just how advisable this attitude to aircraft loading weight was.

Before proceeding any further, I should explain that I was not really an accountant. I was actually an economics student who had worked for a year in an accountant's office and half a year for Air Rhodesia and had the rather humble distinction of passing first-year accounting at university. But this was actually enough to be able to make a reasonable impression on manual accounting systems such as those at Air Trans Africa and other small businesses. The finding of the error in the books and the redrafting of the accounts and presenting them to the taxman had taken the month of December, which was a short month anyway and I now had most of January to put some rudimentary accounting procedures into place. Bob and Iris Nesbit were willing learners and they played an important part in the administration of the organisation. By the end of January I had to return to university to continue with my economics and political science degree, but I enjoyed working with Air Trans Africa sufficiently for me to spend all the rest of my vacations there and I also came back and worked with the company for two years after I graduated.

The Air Trans Africa family

It is difficult to refer to the bunch of people who were employed by Jack Malloch as anything else other than a sort of complicated and rather dysfunctional family in that a number of people did not get on all that well with one another. There were about 20 staff in total. The air crew were mostly British, Rhodesian and South African, a number of whom had served in the RAF or RRAF and were qualified to fly a range of propeller aircraft. There were 6 or 7 office wallahs and about 4 or 5 labourers. A characteristic of this group of people was that most of them rarely did any work – they were on long term stand by. At least they didn't fly for quite a lot of the time during the period I am describing. As mentioned previously, shortly before I arrived at Air Trans Africa, Jack had been running a passenger charter business between Salisbury and a number of different cities in Europe. He had leased what some people had referred to as elderly passenger planes, although in reality they were not that old at all. However they were not jet aircraft and the public were increasingly expecting to fly long distances in jets such as the Boeing 707 or the DC-8 both of which came into service in 1958.

Jack's aircraft were piston engine planes designed and built in the years leading up to commercial jet propulsion. Piston engines are intrinsically less reliable than jet engines and the engines designed and built for the Lockheed Super Constellation and the Douglas McDonald DC-7 pushed the piston engine technology to its limit. Thus there was a greater need for more maintenance and spares backup and attention than Jack was able to provide.

The trouble of course was that some particular airplanes and engines were intrinsically more unreliable than others and during this period Jack had little luck on the reliability front. It is important to say that reliability was seen as quite a different issue to safety.

There wasn't the slightest suggestion that any of these planes were unsafe to fly. All Jack's airplanes, except the Dove, had four engines and so even with one engine failure or perhaps even two, there would not necessarily be a catastrophic crash. I certainly relished the few opportunities I was offered to fly in Jack's fleet.

From the passenger charter perspective, Jack's marketing efforts in Salisbury had been relatively successful and he had sent a number of planeloads of people on British and European holidays. However a number of these planes had broken down on route or had been unable to fly back to Salisbury without very substantial repairs and maintenance. This inevitably caused the crews considerable embarrassment as well as the company back home, but it was the crews who had to face the passengers on the ground and that had been difficult.

A DC-7C of the type used by Jack in his passenger charter business to Europe.
Source: http://commons.wikimedia.org/wiki/File:Douglas_DC-7C_Seven_Seas_AN1468562.jpg

Engine failure had been the main issue. Whether or not it was legally required, Jack felt obliged to accommodate stranded passengers in hotels and supplied them with food etc., for the duration of their additional and unwanted stay abroad. In addition he had to find the money to acquire the necessary components to make the aircraft serviceable. This consumed very large amounts of funds and it was these technical problems more than anything else which nearly brought Air Trans Africa to financial ruin. When I arrived in the company in late 1966 the passenger business for Jack was over.

Everyone in Air Trans Africa said that they wanted nothing more to do with passengers. Freight would be the future of the business. I often heard the mantra, "Freight can't talk back at you". Time and again it was said that "Freight can't complain when the flight is late. It can't argue about the accommodation you are offering or the meals that you are supplying."

> The DC-7 has been described as the best three engine aircraft of its day. This is a way of saying that the engines were not reliable, and that meant it was an inappropriate aircraft with which to run a passenger service from Rhodesia to Europe, especially by a small company such as Air Trans Africa that did not have the resources behind it to fund the huge costs incurred when passengers were stranded.

But Jack was looking around for other ways of earning a living from flying airplanes and it is true that he did not return to flying passengers for quite a few years. But return he did and he even ran a scheduled passenger service in a Lockheed Super Constellation between Salisbury and Windhoek.

By the way, it is interesting to note that there was little talk of any of the stranded passengers trying to sue the airline. They seemed to have taken their misfortune somewhat philosophically, although I expect that this was to a material extent due to the rather generous way in which Jack had treated them when they were stranded. These passengers also probably realised that at the end of this passenger flying episode, Air Trans Africa was on the verge of bankruptcy and they would have got nothing for their trouble. There was also no feeling in the organisation that Jack had not been wise in his choice of aircraft. It seemed that it was just taken for granted that airplanes like these would break down in inconvenient places and that everyone had to take it in their stride. With my passenger's hat on I found this rather curious.

With no passenger services Air Trans Africa did not need in-flight assistants, or to use the old language, air hostesses, nor did they need as many pilots or flight engineers, for that matter. But Jack was not good at laying people off and for quite some time there were a number of employees who came into the offices of Air Trans Africa from time to time but who did not have any work to do. These people chatted to their friends and then went home. Those of us working in the office on accounting and administration were very hard pressed to bring the accounting up to date as quickly as possible and there was a substantial disconnect between the underemployed crew and the harassed office workers. The underemployed crew occasionally showed their personal frustration in amusing ways. On one occasion while I was reviewing documents related to Malawi Air Freighters, or MAF for short, one of the captains who was paying a social visit to the office idly asked me what I was working on. I replied, "I am sorting out the corporate registration for MAF and what we need to do in Blantyre". "Oh", said he, "That's the new company name then, *Malloch's Air Force!*" "No", said one of the underemployed flight attendants with some passion in her voice, "MAF doesn't mean Malloch's Air Force; it stands for Malloch's Air Farce!" This was not a joke which was made openly and I did not hear it repeated again.

I was fascinated by the continued underemployment of so many people, especially as I was party to the payroll figures and knew how much they were earning – and some of them were on really good salaries. In fact, as there was virtually no money in the Air Trans Africa bank account, few people were actually paid more than a small fraction of their normal salary. However everyone trusted Jack to produce the money in the end and so he did. Jack himself was taking a modest salary and he was paying some of the captains nearly as much money as he was taking himself from the business. But Jack wasn't getting any personal cash from the business either. I more than once suggested to him that he should speak to the non-working crew members about putting some of them onto a retainer which would not be as expensive as paying them a full salary. In general Jack did not think much of this idea as he wanted his people to be there ready and waiting when he needed them.

It has always amazed me how the various people involved were able to get by on only small token payments from Air Trans Africa for months on end. There was never a suggestion that they had taken part-time jobs nor were there any clues given that their wives were working to support them. I guess that they had been paid so well by Jack in the past that they had substantial savings which saw them over these very lean times. It was almost unheard of for anyone to resign from Air Trans Africa.

Some of the main characters in the airline were the Chief Pilot, the Chief Flight Engineer, and the Head of Engineering (on the ground). Both the Chief Pilot and the Head of Engineering were mature men, some might say old men. No one knew their ages for sure but they were certainly older than Jack. Neither of them enjoyed great health and it is unlikely that they would have been employed anywhere else. The Chief Pilot, a title which was given to the oldest pilot, was overweight and wore a thick pair of spectacles. He waddled along rather than walked. There was a joke in the office that he knew his way around Africa so well that he could fly even if he had to use a white stick. And indeed he did fly extensively into all sorts of interesting places in Africa and beyond. The Chief Flight Engineer was a much younger man with older engineers in his team and was well respected as he had flown for a number of companies around the world. He gave the impression that he was waiting for something more interesting to turn up, and so it did. The Head of Engineering came and went from the office adjacent to the hangar without having much to say to anyone else. Sometimes it was said that the Head of Engineering was actually the invisible man. With the airplanes being grounded at this time he also had little to do. He was concerned with the authenticity of spares. Jack had famously come back to Salisbury with quantities of spare parts which he had acquired in various parts of the world, but which did not necessarily have all the documentation normally expected so engineering had to ensure that these components were carefully inspected and that their condition was good enough to have them returned to use. The airframes of cannibalised aircraft can be seen at many airports in Africa where components have been rescued from the scrap heap for recycling after inspection and overhaul where necessary. Over the years Jack had accumulated a fair amount of these components and thus on paper the spare part inventory of Air Trans Africa was large. There was a securely locked component store room in the hangar which contained a material number of expensive spares and which was looked after by the only black man who worked for Air Trans Africa who was not a labourer. This man, whose name was Edward, had been able to stay at school into his teenage years and thus he was literate and had some numerical skills as well, which enabled him to perform a very useful function as the component store keeper in the engineering section of the business. He was especially involved with the record keeping in the component stores which is a vital part of the operation of an airline.

There were not many active airplanes in the company fleet at that time and whatever servicing was done was mostly conducted abroad. However the Head of Engineering's presence in the Air Trans Africa team was certainly important to Jack.

Air Trans Africa had a Commercial Manager who was a charming gentleman who had kissed the Blarney Stone, many times over. Since the collapse of the passenger charter business he did not really have much of a function, but he was one of Jack's old stalwarts and had become part of the furniture. His contribution to the organisation was not obvious and his presence was somewhat resented by the others. He stayed on as it was not clear that he would have easily found another job elsewhere.

One of the longest serving members of Jack's team was Bob Nesbit. Bob had been with Jack from the days of Fish Air and by now Bob could not see himself doing anything else with his life other than working for Jack Malloch. Bob's wife Iris sometimes spoke of how Jack cast some sort of spell on Bob, but it was clear to me that Bob, who had no paper qualifications and all his professional experience was working with a small airline business, believed that he would not get a job anywhere else. Bob had been an operations manager in earlier days, but now he reinvented himself as an administrator and eventually into what was the cashier or what could be more euphemistically called the treasurer. His wife Iris came to the office to lend a hand in shifting the backlog of paper work which had accumulated since the collapse of the passenger service. Iris Nesbit was an interesting woman in a number of respects. She was hardly more than five foot tall and probably weighed only 40 kilos. Although she had spent most of her life in Rhodesia she had been born in Mozambique of Portuguese stock. However she was very strong willed and terrorised all the crews in the way that she made them account for every penny they spent in their expense claims. Iris wanted receipts for everything. If a crew member bought a newspaper and charged it to his expense account Iris wanted to know why. She was resented by some of the crew for her attitude towards this which was seen by them as penny pinching. Iris kept Jack well informed as to who was *stretching a point* with their expenses and who was not. She claimed that Jack had a long memory when it came to registering who had the best interests of Air Trans Africa at heart. As she was only a part-timer at Air Trans Africa I felt she had a more objective view of the operation. Although completely loyal to Jack she could be quite critical of how the firm was run especially when Jack was away flying and of course Jack was away quite a lot of the time. Iris was the first to point out to me Jack's extraordinary leadership skills which explain at least in part how the crew stuck with him even when they were not being paid for such a long period. Iris was of the view that if a man worked for Jack for a year or so then he was Jack's for life. This was probably not entirely true.

Other employees of Air Trans Africa consisted of a small contingency of black labourers. They worked at cleaning the aircraft and the environs of the hangar. At the end of 1966 and the beginning of 1967 there was little for them to do but they stayed on the payroll and the Head of Engineering found things to occupy them. The pay for black people was low. In fact, coming to think of it Air Trans Africa did not pay any of its office staff particularly well including Jack himself who took a modest salary from the firm. But the labourers' small wage package was considered a priority and somehow Bob Nesbit found some money to pay them each month.

Bob Nesbit ran a micro-finance operation for the black staff. Because of their low pay black staff always had problems when a sizeable amount of money was required such as they might need for a wedding or for a funeral or something similar. When this happened they came to see Bob who would always find some money for them and then reclaim it back on their pay day in easy instalments. Of course there was no question of interest being charged and often the instalments were missed. I was impressed at the amount of trouble Bob went to in order to be helpful in this respect.

But not everyone was helpful to the black staff. I arrived at the office one Monday morning to be greeted with the news that Edward, our component store keeper, was in jail. It appeared that on leaving the airport on the Friday evening Edward had been stopped by the security people and his car boot was searched. In the boot was a broken aircraft engine cylinder. It was simply scrap metal. When questioned about why he had this piece of metal in his car Edward replied that he had asked Captain Jack if he could have the scrap metal and he had received permission to take it away as it had no practical use. The security people were not satisfied with this and the BSAP (British South Africa Police) were called. At this particular moment Jack was away.

For some reason the BSAP got in touch with the Commercial Manager who said that he had no reason to believe that Captain Malloch would have given this broken component to Edward. On the strength of this Edward was arrested and locked up in the police cells in Manica Road.

I was completely perplexed by these events and when Bob Nesbit arrived it was decided that I should go into town and talk to the BSAP. I found the Duty Sergeant and introduced myself. At this stage I had the title of Company Secretary of Air Trans Africa and in this role I stated that I had no reason to believe that Jack Malloch had not given Edward permission to take this rather valueless broken aircraft engine cylinder. I pointed out that Edward had a good job and that good jobs were hard to come by and that Edward was not going to jeopardise this job for a few shillings worth of scrap metal.

I was taken to the cells where Edward was handed over to me. What a pathetic sight to see this slightly built man in prison uniform.

On his return Jack was just as perplexed about this incident as anyone else.

The main financial affairs of the Salisbury office were not complex, but there was quite a lot of sorting out to be done with regard to aircrew expenses when they were overseas and this always took a long time. There was also the fact that Jack had at one time thought that he would run an airline based in Malawi and he had opened a number of corporate entities in that country. There was a similar situation in Zambia and there was even an office with a representative in Johannesburg. All of these legal and financial entities needed to be sorted out and they were time-consuming and tedious. On paper Air Trans Africa was the centre of a substantial commercial network of aircraft operating interests.

Although Salisbury was the capital of Southern Rhodesia and thus a city it was really a small town. With an altitude of nearly 5,000 feet above sea level it was seldom uncomfortably hot and it was not ever really cold. As far as cities go it was a gem of a place with an especially attractive central square. On the square were some of the most important buildings in the country including the cathedral, the national newspaper, the only luxury hotel in Salisbury and the meeting place of the really important people in the country – the Salisbury Club. In Spring the city became a mass of purple as thousands of Jacaranda trees blossomed in the city's avenues.

Cecil Square, the central square in Salisbury was always beautifully manicured.
Source:http://commons.wikimedia.org/wiki/File:Anglican_Cathedral,_Salisbury_Rhodesia_ca1975_6899218321.jpg?uselang=en-gb

The city built on a grid pattern which was easy to understand and traverse: it was clean and well organised. But it was in a number of senses a one-horse town with a narrow perspective on life. It was a modern city which in 1965 was continually being developed and it would have had a population of about 100,000 whites and perhaps half a million blacks. The two great pursuits enjoyed by many members of the white population were sport and socialising. Cricket and rugby were big-time activities and drinking beer was one of the important ways of socialising, and this also applied to those of us working at the airport in the evening. Salisbury Airport was about eight miles out of town, and in 1966 the airport was a Sunday attraction for those who were interested in airplanes. At about 11 am there were three international flights taking off and landing. One could observe the stylish BOAC VC 10 which flew to London. There was a South African Airways Boeing flight at that time and there was another European flight, TAP to Lisbon as I recall which also landed and took off around this time. These events brought sightseers to the airport and the observation terrace would be full of airplane spotters for an hour or so.

TAP was one of the few airlines that flew direct to Europe from Salisbury Airport.

Source: Private collection of Karl Upshon.

Also the restaurant at the airport was particularly good and this brought even more day trippers. But at other times the airport was relatively quiet and the bar and the lounge became a watering hole for some of the employees working at airline companies. Beer was cheap and it flowed freely. If anyone had suggested that there was such a thing as a suitable maximum daily intake for beer, he or she would have been laughed at. There were nights when 10 or 12 bottles of beer were consumed virtually non-stop by several regulars without it appearing to make any impact on their ability to stand up straight. Some of the Air Trans Africa employees were among the regulars at these drinking sessions and it was probably only the short distances and emptiness of the roads between the airport and their homes which prevented any driving incidents. Indeed drinking was a problem in Rhodesia in those days and smoking was a national pastime. As Rhodesia was a major producer of tobacco, cigarettes cost only pennies for a packet of 20.

Jack, who travelled abroad a lot, was an infrequent visitor to these watering holes and when he did visit, he was not much of a drinker. But for some of the others in the company the pub was an important part of the airport and a place to meet and exchange the little gossip which was going around. The need-to-know culture was deeply ingrained in Air Trans Africa and there were very few who openly dared to transgress.

The challenge for airlines and airline entrepreneurs

It has always been difficult to be an airline entrepreneur. This industry attracted considerable attention from its very beginnings in the early years of the 20th century. Spurred on by military use many different types of aircraft were developed and by the 1920s there was a host of aircraft operating companies around the world. By the 1930s there had been a considerable consolidation of airlines with National Carriers becoming the focus of commercial airline activity in many if not most countries.

Flying has always been dangerous. The relationship between man and machine is complex and things go wrong in all sorts of ways. It was therefore understood from the early days that aircraft activity should be regulated by government in order to serve the public interest especially with regard to safety. There were at least three reasons why this regulation was essential, which include the need for assurance that the aircraft were technically sound and thus functioned in the way they were expected to; the need to avoid collision either in the air or on the ground; and the need to have the operation of the airlines conducted in an orderly manner. The aviation industry has always sought continuous innovation and technology of this sort always carries some risk. The stream of technological improvements has been endless but it is not always clear what the implications of these improvements can be and how pilots should manage the challenges they produce. Even today technology can easily baffle the human mind. As recently as June 2009 an Airbus A330-203 flown by Air France fell out of the sky. The cause of this was shown to be a combination of a technological fault and the inappropriate response of a crew who were not fully prepared to handle a problem such as they faced. Anticipating all the consequences of any particular technological innovation has proven to be impossible but the number of problems is generally regarded as having been small and it is regularly held that airline travel is one of the safest forms of transport.

> The Department of Civil Aviation at Salisbury Airport was responsible for the administration and enforcement of airline safety regulations. Everyone had full confidence in the workings of this body and it is correct to say that there were very few untoward incidents. In retrospect aviation was in its infancy and looking back from the 21st century it is not clear that the rules were always enforced as well as they should have been.

With regards to airborne collisions there have been very few such incidents but those that have occurred have been especially horrific. Despite the fact that air traffic control is patchy around the world there has been great success in avoiding collisions. The highest number of fatalities from an airline accident still remains the on-the-ground collision of two Boeing 747s at Tenerife in March 1977 causing the deaths of 583 people. In general, from a safety point of view regulation has been a success but it has resulted in a substantial amount of bureaucracy.

These regulations meant that there was much red tape surrounding airline activities and that it was and still is not an easy matter to obtain the necessary permits to be in this business sector. In fact the set up cost of an airline was generally regarded as enormous and therefore national governments typically became involved, except of course in the USA. The term National Carrier was used to describe these airlines which were generally funded and owned by governments. Most countries had only one National Carrier which operated scheduled passenger services both internally and externally. Many countries had other smaller airlines as well which offered charter services or which operated on more financially difficult routes in which the National Carrier was not interested.

By early 1967 the business prospects for Air Trans Africa which was nothing more than a fledgling micro charter company based in a small landlocked country in the centre of Southern Africa were not looking good. Owning a private airline such as this at that time in the history of aviation was a major challenge with which few organisations or individuals were able to cope.

Most people would have said that Jack was trying to play in a fool's game. Airlines were to a large extent a closed shop due to the combination of government legislation, the bureaucracy associated with the safety issues and the enormous amount of money which is needed to properly fund such an operation. It is certain that Air Trans Africa was not properly capitalised and it was going to be a hard struggle to make a small private airline work.

This was especially true in Southern Africa where there were a small number of busy inter-city routes which made the National Airlines or National Carriers (sometimes referred to as flag carriers) considerable amounts of money. The central problem facing Air Trans Africa was that the airline business was a tightly closed shop in which the National Carrier, i.e. Air Rhodesia, owned by the Government took all the lucrative air traffic for itself. Air Rhodesia was adamant that there should be no competition. They argued that there wasn't adequate demand, on any of their important and generally lucrative routes, to accommodate a second airline. In those days National Carriers insisted that the demand for air travel was not elastic and that more competition leading to better fares would not result in increased demand but rather end up with losses for the National Carriers.

As the Government of Rhodesia owned the National Airline they instructed the Department of Transport who in turn informed the Department of Civil Aviation, which was the body that issued flight licences and permits, not to allow private operator flights. The only exception to this was the charter flight where one person hired an entire airplane to take one party of people to a destination. Organising a charter flight in those days was especially challenging and thus not many charter permits were ever issued. It was this charter flight concept that Jack had used in trying to develop his overseas passenger business. Charter licences were not easy to ob-

> Some of the executives of Air Rhodesia were particularly antagonistic towards Air Trans Africa. They saw the existence of Air Trans Africa as a personal slight on their organisation and went to great lengths to ensure that every obstacle was put in the way of Air Trans Africa obtaining the appropriate permits to operate from Salisbury Airport.

tain and Jack's trouble with the unreliable European flights did not go down well at the Civil Aviation Authority in Salisbury.

In any event the number of people in Rhodesia and South Africa who could afford even a cheap charter flight was quite small in those days so it was unlikely that Jack could make a business out of this. The market for air freight in that part of the world was also very limited indeed. Air Rhodesia and South African Airways were regarded by some as being especially mean in blocking any opportunity for air traffic to go to anyone else in the region.

To make things even more difficult for Jack there was political activity of seismic proportions at this time in Southern Africa.

Africa evolves

Africa is relatively simple to define geographically. It is the second biggest land mass on Earth with the second biggest population. It is bounded by the Mediterranean Sea to the north, the Atlantic Ocean to the west, the Indian Ocean and the Red Sea to the east with a land bridge connecting Africa to Asia in the North Eastern corner. But of course Africa is much more than this. To the Greeks it was the continent where magical Egypt was located. To the Romans it was where the dastardly Carthaginians lived. Africa is where the Moors, who dominated the Iberian Peninsula for centuries, came from. In the early modern era Africa was the place to find the slaves which were needed to work the plantations in the new world. To the modern European nation state it was the place to go to participate in *the scramble for land* in order to build an Empire.

At some point all African countries have been occupied by Europeans, although the Ethiopians point out that they were never conquered and managed to preserve the country's independence during the 19th century scramble for Africa. It was however occupied by the Italians from 1936 to 1941 when the Emperor had to flee the country and take up exile in Great Britain. The British were obliging to the Emperor as his country was being invaded by the Italians who were being far too pally with Nazi Germany.

Huge tracts of Africa were claimed by Europeans as either protectorates and/or colonies often with total disregard of the wishes or the interests of the local peoples. The rivalry of the Europeans for chunks of Africa became so intense that it was necessary to have an orderly carve up of the continent and to this end Otto von Bismarck, first Chancellor of Germany, convened the Berlin Conference of 1884-85 attended by European Governments which had in their possession African colonies. At this conference the boundaries of many African states were set by European Empires. The boundaries so established bore no relationship to the realities of traditional pre-European African politics or culture and were the basis of many difficulties and civil wars which ensued many years later.

The degree to which European presence in Africa was resented varied enormously and was without doubt related to whether local people had been politicised. There was in general a low level of politicisation of Africans until African people were called upon to support European military efforts in the First and the Second World War. It is hard to estimate how many Black and Asian soldiers fought with the allies but there were certainly tens of thousands of such people involved in these war efforts.

Black soldiers, especially those who fought in the Second World War, returned home realising that there were many different types of people in the world of a great variety of political persuasions and attitudes toward Africans. The traditional idea that the white man was boss and the black man was his servant was now too simplistic for the modern world. At about this time a material number of black men began to acquire secondary and tertiary education which both opened up their horizons and gave them the ability to articulate their hopes and aspirations in a way they could not before. To many politicised blacks India's independence in 1947 was a really clear signal that they should be demanding the same freedom.

The Nigerian author Adichie described the feeling of some Africans well when she wrote in her novel Half of a Yellow Sun, "My father's brother fought in Burma and came back filled with one burning question: How come nobody told him before that the white man was not immortal?" Perhaps the word invincible would have been better than immortal.

Africa and Africans were no longer a push over. Clearly the old colonial system had reached its sell by date.

The winds of change

Being based in Salisbury in 1966 made matters related to commercial flying much more difficult for Jack and Air Trans Africa. During his visit to South Africa in 1960 the British Prime Minister Harold MacMillan foretold difficult future events when he described the political African political situation in terms of the "winds of change" which were now blowing throughout Africa. This was not well received in a country where the white minority government had just coined the term apartheid. But by his statement MacMillan was pointing out that the British Empire in Africa was to be dismantled and that the governments of these British territories were to be converted to democracies, one-man-one-vote regimes, and thus handed over to the management of local people.

Harold MacMillan, the great white chief from the North, wearing some African garb, brings the message of the winds of change to an unreceptive South Africa.

Source:http://commons.wikimedia.org/wiki/File:The_National_Archives_U_CO_10 69-1-5.jpg

Harold MacMillan was not an aristocrat but he certainly had an aristocratic tone of voice and manner and using him to convey the message that the mother country no longer wanted the colonies was not going to go down well in certain parts of Africa. He was a man in a suit whose opinion did not necessarily have that much relevance to the people in power locally. It was now 15 years since the end of the Second World War; a new generation of politicians with quite a different outlook were managing Rhodesia and South Africa and the concerns of the *mother country* now seemed far away.

But this message delivered by MacMillan should not have been a surprise to anyone in the British Empire as it was generally well recognised that the Empire had reached its zenith some time before (it has been claimed that the zenith of the empire was the crowning of Queens Victoria as Empress of India in 1876) and was on a path of steady decline. It is sometimes debated as to when the zenith of British power and influence was achieved and there is considerable disagreement about this. Some argue that it was at the Battle of Waterloo while others claim that it was during the Crimean War. What is generally recognised is that Great Britain's difficulty in subduing two small republics in Southern Africa in what is called the Second Anglo-Boer War, was a surprise to the world and foretold of a future in which the might of Britannia was going to be called into question in her colonies.

Although perhaps they should have been, these Boer fighters were not scared of the might of the British Empire.
Source:http://commons.wikimedia.org/wiki/File:The_Second_Boer_War,_1899-1902_Q68470.jpg?uselang=en-gb

After all, in this war the Imperial Army had to a large extent only faced a relatively rag-tag bunch of commandos whose day jobs had been tending to the routine of farm life. This does not mean that the Boers were not a deadly fighting force. In fairness there were some professional Boer soldiers and some European powers supplied them with modern weapons but for the most part the Boers fought as bands of guerrillas.

There were also some groups of Irish and American fighters who wanted another chance to fight against what they regarded as their natural foe. It was not yet realised how such warfare could be countered. Even today professional armies have difficulty when faced by guerrillas. The cost of the war to the Empire was estimated as exceeding £200 million and there had been more than 100,000 British and Colonial casualties. As a result this war took three years to conclude and only came to an end after much hardship to the Afrikaners including women and children being confined in camps, a scorched earth policy and men being deported to Ceylon and Patagonia. No British conflict since 1815 had been so prolific in lives and in treasure.

The authors of the Atlantic Charter.
Source:http://commons.wikimedia.org/wiki/File:Prince_of_Wales-5.jpg

Twenty years later the Empire began to unravel more seriously with the British having to partition the island of Ireland, allowing the Republicans in the South to establish the Irish Free State as a first step to becoming a sovereign republic. This was perceived as a major crack in British Imperial interests which had become necessary despite the draconian way the Irish rebellion had been suppressed in 1916 and the inability of the Black and Tans to illuminate the growing anti-British sentiment in the country. The struggle with the Irish was an old one which depending on one's point of view can be said to have begun in 1170 with the landing of Strong Bow, a Norman knight in Ireland. Of course there was no notion of a British Empire in those days and these conquerors in the 12th century didn't speak English. The Irish remained troublesome for the 700 intervening years and eventually a different solution was sought. However the partition of the country and the freedom thus offered to the Republicans signalled to the other subject peoples of the Empire that freedom was possible.

Great Britain was not alone in the disintegration of its Empire. France would grant independence to most of its African possessions by the end of 1960 and in this year the Belgians withdrew from the Belgian Congo leaving behind a most unsatisfactory situation leading to some of the worst examples of civil unrest on the continent. The Belgians' record in Africa may well be the worst of all the colonial powers with an especially cruel regime for which they did not really received the criticism they deserved.

By 1960 the age of Empires was largely if not entirely over. The notion that white men should govern in Africa was now an antiquated one and the only question was when and how would power be transferred to the local or indigenous people. Great Britain and France did not decide to liberate their African possessions because of a Road to Damascus type conversion in which they realised the immorality and injustice of their behaviour in their colonies. It had become increasingly difficult and enormously expensive to maintain the necessary military presence in the colonies which was required to ensure the compliance of the locals and safety of the colonialists. In some cases it was simply impossible.

Perhaps the war or perhaps better described as the "struggle" against the Mau Mau in Kenya fought between 1952 and 1960 is a prime example of this within the British sphere of influence in Africa. Although most people would say that the British defeated the Mau Mau the cost of this war in terms of lives, treasure and especially British prestige was actually substantial. Wars against indigenous people are always dirty affairs and there are accusations of massacres from both sides. In addition there are claims against the British forces who are accused of torture and

> The expense of maintenance is said by some to have been at the heart of the dissolution of the empire. Great Britain is reported to have been bankrupted by the costs of the two World Wars. And although this is probably true in at least some sense, it was also the cost of creating the welfare society which impacted the way Great Britain was to be seen as a world power. It is difficult to find the funds for the Health, Education and Social Policies as well as keep a significant standing army to police the empire.

these claims have been given a sympathetic hearing in British courts in 2012.

The French, of course, had already been humiliated in Indochina with their defeat at the Battle of Dien Bien Phu in 1954. The end of empire is of course a very difficult time for both the colonialists and the "mother country" and although the French coped well in a number of cases in Africa their attitude in Algeria resulted in enormous damage and trauma. The French had only been in Algeria since 1830 but they perceived this piece of North Africa to be an integral part of France itself. Their control of this huge country was simply not sustainable in the second half of the 20th century. It is estimated that as many as one and a half million people died in the Algerian War and it was not until Charles de Gaulle masterminded or some would say imposed the French withdrawal that peace was restored. This in turn led to bitter disputes, some would argue almost leading to a civil war, within France itself.

Another important issue which came into play at this time was an increasing acceptance of the principle of self determination for the peoples of the world. Some argue that this concept can be traced back to the Atlantic Charter which was signed during the Second World War in 1941. This "treaty" was agreed by Franklin D. Roosevelt, President of the United States of America, and Winston Churchill, Prime Minister of the United Kingdom. However to say that this was their brainchild is not strictly correct as self determination is actually one of the 14 Points articulated by Woodrow Wilson in the final months of the First World War.

The concept of self determination was a relatively new one at this time and it is sometimes seen as the intellectual justification for the dissolution of the Austro-Hungarian and Ottoman Empires. Both of these Empires were on the losing side of the First World War and had many subjugated peoples within their borders who wanted their independence and it was in the direct interest of the victors to see these Empires broken up. And so it was that a number of new nation states came into existence after this war. But self determination was not applied in an even handed way as the wishes of the German speaking peoples were clearly ignored. Thus it was said that the Wilsonian 14 Points, proclaimed in January 1918, were seen by some at the time as a statement of political aspiration. But others argued that it was a question of political expediency; other groups saw the 14 Points as a confidence trick to encourage Germany to give up their

Atlantic Charter- Principal Points

- no territorial gains for the United States or the United Kingdom;
- the wishes of the peoples concerned to influence any territorial adjustments;
- all people were to have a right to self-determination;
- lowered trade barriers;
- worldwide economic cooperation and social advancement;
- work towards freedom of want and fear;
- freedom of the seas;
- disarmament of aggressor nations, and general reduction of arms.

Several of these mitigated the power and influence of the British and French Empires find the funds for the Health, Education and Social Policies as well as keep a significant standing army to police the empire.

war efforts and seek surrender or as it turned out armistice. In the end there was not much effort made to implement many of the 14 Points.

The Atlantic Charter reiterated self determination and gave it additional credibility, authority and prominence. The motivation for self determination at this point in history was clearly different. There were no defeated Empires, at least in the Western Hemisphere, to be dissolved. The momentum for self determination came from the United States which was not a country famous for the sensitive treatment of its own citizens. Segregation which severally prejudiced the life opportunities of black and first nation citizens of the country was the order of the day in the Southern States of the USA and there had been little political appetite among the Federal Government institutions to correct this situation. Some observers say that there was no moral underpinning of the Atlantic Charter but that it was simply an economic-political stratagem or device.

Empires are essentially clubs in which non-members cannot play a meaningful role. By 1940 the USA knew that it had a worldwide economic role to play and it could not do this effectively while such large parts of the world were dominated by the British and the French Empires. Thus the Atlantic Charter may be seen as the declaration that the British and French Empires would have to come to an end and that the white man's influence in Asia and Africa would soon be over. It is sometimes suggested that Churchill did not fully realise this when he subscribed to this Charter.

Back in Africa

However not everyone saw the withdrawal of white peoples' influence from South Africa as an appropriate tactic. In the first place the Portuguese also had an active Empire. This Empire has been described as the oldest of the European Empires and in its heyday Portugal had extensive territories all over the world. By the 20th century the Portuguese Empire had been whittled down and in Africa there were two small territories which went by the names of Guinea Bissau and Equatorial Guinea, two sets of islands and two large tracts of land called Angola and Mozambique. At the time of the withdrawal of the French and the British winds-of-change speech the Portuguese were not of a mind to give up these overseas territories and it was going to take a revolution in Portugal and several years of blood-soaked conflict in the colonies before they decided to quit.

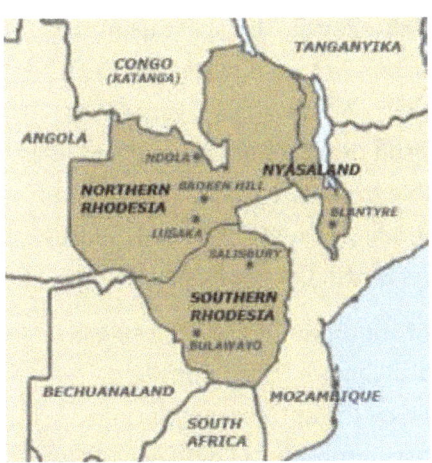

The Central African Federation. A political entity with no power or influence which lasted a very short time. It did not have the support of the local people and was thus not viable.
Source:http://commons.wikimedia.org/wiki/File:Federation_rhodesia_nyasaland.png

Meanwhile South Africa, which was by far the most industrially developed country in Africa, was under the control of a white Afrikaner minority government who believed that it had an almost divine right to govern not only itself but also the other ethnic groups within its boundaries. Afrikaners saw themselves as white Africans whose roots in Africa went back in many cases some hundreds of years or more. They resented interference from any outsiders especially the British who had been the enemy of the Boer Republics at the turn of the 20th century. They were not going to willingly give any significant political power to local people within their country. It is worth mentioning that South Africa had been given by a League of Nations mandate the administration of the German South-West Africa former colony which it administered much like any of its other provinces where it operated an apartheid regime.

South Africa had dominion status which meant that it was an autonomous political entity within the British Empire and as such it had full legal powers over all its own affairs. This allowed the South African Nationalist Government to hold a referendum of white only voters on the question of becoming a republic independent of Great Britain. The electorate supported the idea of becoming a republic with a vote of 52% in favour and 48% against. This split meant that Afrikaans speaking South Africans were in favour of the country becoming a republic and English speaking South African wanted the county to remain as it was. As a result of this referendum the South African Government was legally able to declare itself a republic and to thus break all ties with Great Britain which it did in 1961. Shortly thereafter South Africa also left the British Commonwealth.

North of South Africa the colony of Southern Rhodesia formed in 1923 was a special case in the British Empire. This colony was formed out of territories controlled by the entrepreneurial and para-military entity called the British South Africa Company and was established as a self-governing colony with substantial autonomy on the model of the dominions. But it did not have formal dominion status. It was therefore not legally autonomous in the same way that South Africa was. Although they were not formally applied, the Imperial authorities in London had retained direct powers over the affairs of the colony and therefore it could not make any changes to its constitution without the express permission of London. It was largely due to this ambiguity whereby Southern Rhodesia was treated as though it were a dominion whilst not technically being one that was to be at the root of the trouble which lay ahead.

Rhodesians had certainly played an important role in World War Two and this was recognised in several ways including the closeness of the colonial army to that of the mother country.

Monty inspects Rhodesian troops in 1947.
Source:http://commons.wikimedia.org/wiki/File:Montgomery_inspects_Ro yal_Rhodesia_Regiment_guard_of_honour_1947.jpg?uselang=en-gb

Between 1953 and 1963 Southern Rhodesia joined with Northern Rhodesia and Nyasaland to form the Central African Federation. The Central African Federation then consisted of an area approximately equal to France, Germany and Italy. The intention in setting up this vast political entity was that the Central African Federation would operate as a sort of compromise between African National aspirations and Colonialist interests. This was the 20th century equivalent of the Conference of Berlin and was clearly doomed to fail. This was another example of the self delusion of Imperial politicians who wanted to see the prolongation of white influence in Africa but who realised that the current situation was untenable. The thinking was that a form of qualified franchise could be used to keep white influence alive for many years to come. But this was not possible as black politicians saw whites as transient settlers who could not be trusted to act in the best interests of all the people and the black politicians felt that they were perfectly capable of running their own countries themselves. The establishment of fully independent African states ruled by majority voting was the only acceptable way forward to the majority of black politicians.

This Federation came to an end in 1964 when Northern Rhodesia was given its independence and changed its name to Zambia. Nyasaland immediately followed suit becoming Malawi. Southern Rhodesia then led by the Rhodesian Front, a political party which represented white interests, changed the name of the country to Rhodesia and believed that it was also entitled to full independence under its limited franchise constitution. The Rhodesian Front objected to the notion of a one-man one-vote election as suggested by Great Britain on the grounds that the black population still needed white leadership. However London did not see the situation in the same way and led by Harold Wilson the British insisted that Rhodesian independence was contingent on one-man one-vote majority rule being established in the country. No independence before majority rule, which was abbreviated as NIBMAR, became a slogan used by those opposed to the concept of a qualified franchise proposed by the Rhodesians.

After a short period of intense negotiation which produced no useful result the Rhodesia Government of Ian Douglas Smith decided to break away and unilaterally declared independence from Great Britain on November 11, 1965. This was an enormous embarrassment to London which was expected by various members of the

Commonwealth to quash this rebellion by force in the same way that the British had put down other rebellions before.

Ian Smith and Harold Wilson tried to find common ground between colonial values and African nationalist aspirations.
Source: http://commons.wikimedia.org/wiki/File:Smith_et_Wilson.jpg

The British notion of majority rule before independence for the colony was unacceptable to the government in Salisbury and the rebels decided that Rhodesia did not need to comply with the wishes of the former Imperial Motherland. Ian Smith regularly claimed to be the instrument of Western Christian values in Africa and voiced the view that there would not be majority rule in Rhodesia during his life time. He claimed to have the support of the tribal leaders who he said were opposed to the African nationalists. This was of course an exercise in self-deception on a grand scale which can only be concocted by politicians who have run out of options and justifications for their actions. Smith's pronouncements should not be regarded as cynically as Richard Nixon's "There will be no white wash at the White House" but their effect was fairly similar.

A new flag was established and Rhodesia went about trying to establish itself as a legitimate member of the community of nations.

Source: http://commons.wikimedia.org/wiki/File:Smith_Dinner.jpg

Of course the Imperial bosses in London regarded Ian Smith's declaration of independence as illegal, and so applied a number of punitive sanctions. They expelled Rhodesia from the sterling area which was intended to undermine the Rhodesian currency and thus wreck the economy. Wilson famously claimed that these sanctions would bring Rhodesia to its knees in a matter of months if not weeks and this claim was as self-delusionary as Ian Smith's no black government in his lifetime was. There was talk, especially by black Commonwealth leaders of the necessity for immediate military intervention to bring the rebels to heel but it wasn't clear that this was a serious suggestion. Although the Rhodesia military was small to miniscule, relative to the British Army, the location of the country was such that it would have taken an enormous amount of resources to bring an adequate fighting force against the rebel country. Some Rhodesians asserted that the British Army would mutiny before they would fight against their kith and kin. It is hard to believe that a mutiny such as this could have come to pass but this

> It is striking how differently Great Britain treated South Africa and Rhodesia on the independence issue. There is little disagreement that apartheid treated South Africa's indigenous peoples much more harshly and unfairly than the form of government in Rhodesia. Despite this South Africa was allowed to become an independent state and pursue whatever policies it wished while Rhodesia was obliged to bow to the dictates of London.

hypothesis was never tested. On Wilson's instructions a study was conducted by the British military as to the feasibility of an armed intervention in Rhodesia and it was decided that the resources required were not available. Maybe deep in the British subconscious there was a memory of the previous little war in South Africa i.e. the Boer War which really got out of hand.

There was however a minor involvement of British military power through the use of the Royal Navy.

HMS Ark Royal which was on the Beira Patrol.

Source:http://commons.wikimedia.org/wiki/File:17_HMS_Ark_Royal_North_Atlantic_July_76.jpg

A Beira Patrol was established using two or three naval vessels including a couple of frigates and support from an aircraft carrier. It was the intention of this patrol to cut off the supply of petroleum through the Mozambique port of Beira. This tactic was not effective and was eventually abandoned.

> The Smith Government argued that voting rights should be based on merit. There should be education qualifications and property rights attached to the privilege of voting. This effectively excluded many black people from voting as they simply did not meet the required level of qualification. This was the basis of Smith's claim that there would not be a black government in his life time. The black population had a lot of catching up to do to qualify for a vote in Smith's proposed system.

Behind the scenes there was some considerable debate in Great Britain about the appropriateness of sanctions. Sanctions would not only hurt Rhodesia but would also impact negatively on the Mother country and anything that would affect jobs was not good news for a political party even at that time. There was the question of how sanctions could be enforced. It is almost impossible to force another country to impose sanctions against a third party. Despite all the international agreements to enforce sanctions there were many countries which ignored their own agreements in this respect.

However negotiations between Great Britain and the Rhodesian rebels did continue with two high profile meetings at Gibraltar and in the Mediterranean Sea - I guess this location was used because it was between Europe and Africa - with Ian Smith and Harold Wilson on the cruiser the HMS Tiger and the destroyer HMS Fearless. Neither of these meetings resolved any of the issues and by 1968 Great Britain approached the United Nations to adopt general sanctions against the rebel colony. These sanctions included diplomatic relations, military aid, and international transportation and communication. According to the UN Resolution any country which continued to trade with Rhodesia illegally could itself be subject to economic sanctions by the Security Council.

It is clear that Smith and his colleagues in the Rhodesian Front did not expect there to be such a strong negative reaction in London to his unilateral declaration of independence. The Rhodesian Government often talked about how the British were their kith and kin and how they deserved the support of Great Britain rather than its condemnation. After all, the Rhodesians argued, they had fought and had given lives for Great Britain in two World Wars earlier that century. In fact on a per capita basis Rhodesia had contributed more men to the Second World War effort than anyone else in the British Empire including the Mother country itself.

The undertone of the Rhodesian argument was that they should have been treated in the same way as the South Africans were. Although Rhodesia was not de jure a dominion it was de facto one and this should have been recognised and honoured by the men in suits in London. But London knew that the white man's rule in Africa was over and wanted to be on the side of the future.

As it turned out Ian Smith's unilateral declaration produced 15 more years of white control whereas the South African apartheid republic managed to survive for almost 50 years in total. However in both cases it was reasonably clear to anyone who was prepared to take a longer view of historical trends that in the end majority rule would have to come about and the question was how long could this reality be avoided and at what cost in lives and treasure. By the nature of their function politicians are seldom if ever equipped to think much ahead of their term of office or the immediate circumstances which are presenting themselves to them.

The table below shows the names of the countries in Southern Africa and the dates of their independence.

Country	Land Mass square miles in thousand	Date of Independence
Angola	481	11 November 1974
Botswana	225	30 September 1966
Lesotho	13	4 October 1966
Malawi	46	6 July 1964
Mozambique	309	25 June 1975
Namibia	318	21 March 1990
Rhodesia	151	11 November 1965
South Africa – Apartheid Republic	471	31 May 1961
South Africa – Democratic Republic	471	31 May 1994
Swaziland	6	6 September 1968
Zambia	290	24 October 1964
Zimbabwe	151	18 April 1980

Note how Zambia and Malawi had their independence a year or more before Rhodesia's declaration of independence.

Jack and Nigeria

Although several thousand miles to the north, Nigeria was to play a very important role in Jack's life and in the development of Air Trans Africa. Being prepared to fly in war zones was one of the most defining characteristics of Jack's career and the Nigerian civil war gave him an excellent opportunity in this regard.

Regions of Nigeria.
Source:http://commons.wikimedia.org/wiki/File:Nigeria_1960-1963.png

Nigeria like most other African countries was created out of many different groups of people who were put together into one administrative unit for the convenience of an external power which in this case was Great Britain.

The country had been established in 1914 after boundaries had been agreed by Great Britain and Germany and when various smaller protectorates were consolidated to establish the Colony and Protectorate of Nigeria. It is hard to know just how many different ethnic or cultural groups there were in Nigeria when it obtained its independence from Great Britain in 1960. It is said that the country has 50 languages and about 250 dialects. Some sources claim that there were several hundred ethnic groups but at independence the country was divided into three states with a federal republican constitution for the country as a whole. The three states were Northern Nigeria, Western Nigeria and Eastern Nigeria.

Northern Nigeria was by far the biggest in area and population. The dominant group there were the Hausa and the political authority was exercised by the Northern People's Congress. The main group in the Western Region were the Yoruba and their political party was the Action Group. In Eastern Nigeria the Igbo were the primary group and their political organisation was The National Council of Nigeria and the Cameroons.

There were significant economic, political and social differences between the cultures of these three regions and moulding them into one country was problematic. The constitution proposed by the

British at independence meant that the Northern Region was effectively in control of the country. Neither the Yoruba nor the Igbo appreciated this arrangement, although the Yoruba who were more culturally aligned to the Hausa were not as distressed about this as the Igbo. It is said that the Igbo went along with this situation believing they could eventually change the constitution.

The Nigerian Independence Day October 1, 1960 was celebrated with visiting dignitaries from around the world. It was a happy day for the people of Nigeria who were glad to see the end of British rule.

Great Britain left Nigeria having given it the most fabulous gift it could – the Westminster form of parliamentary government!

In 1960 and perhaps even today there are those who believe that the Westminster system of parliamentary government is the best any country could have. Unfortunately the record of this system bringing stability to countries in Africa is not good. Westminster parliamentary government requires that there should be a relatively homogeneous population which shares culture, values and aspirations.

Because Nigeria was composed of three significantly different regions put together for the convenience of Great Britain the peoples of this country had little in common with regard to culture, values and aspirations. Furthermore Northern Nigeria, being so much bigger than the other two states, dominated the political processes in the country. It is rather surprising that the Yoruba and Igbo accepted independence under these conditions but it appears their dislike for being a British colony was greater than their ability to foresee the problems which would lie ahead. They jumped out of the British frying pan into the Federal Nigerian fire.

In the early years of the First Nigerian Republic there appears to have been considerable corruption which undermined the confidence of the people in their political processes. When the first election after independence took place there were strong rumours of extensive ballot box fixing.

The emergence of Biafra

Deep dissatisfaction with the political system among the ordinary people led to junior officers masterminding a military a coup in January 1966. Most of the coup plotters were Igbo. The coup itself was short lived as senior members of the military with a counter coup took over the federal government. An extended period of extreme political disarray ensued in which thousands of Igbo were killed. There was a considerable amount of suspicion in Nigeria that Igbo had ambitions which were beyond the interests of their own region and this was resented in a number of quarters. From an Igbo point of view they knew that they were not generally liked in other parts of Nigeria and thus they did not want to be locked into an artificial political entity created by the British.

These tensions between the Igbo and the rest of the country mounted and eventually led to Eastern Nigeria declaring itself to be an independent country and renaming itself Biafra.

In the time honoured tradition of not allowing part of your country to succeed from the union, the balance of the original Nigerian Federation initiated a police action against the rebels and this constituted the opening gambit in the Nigerian Civil War which was also known as the Biafran War. There is certainly deep irony in calling this military move "police action"! This brutal war began on July 6, 1967 and lasted until January 15, 1970. These two and a half years resulted in the death of about 50,000 combatants and between two and three million civilians. How could a civil war between two non-industrial groups of people have lasted so long and caused so much hardship? The Nigerians were backed by Great Britain who did not want to admit that their model of democracy may not have been right for Nigeria. Other countries such as the Soviet Union, Egypt, Poland and Hungary supported the Federal army probably because there were issues related to oil rights in Eastern Nigeria. On the other side the Biafrans were supported by France, Portugal, South Africa and Rhodesia and to some extent the USA and Canada. Once again the oil issue was important but in the case of Rhodesia they saw Biafra for what it was - a rebel state much as themselves and this encouraged them to give this new would-be county some support.

France was by far the biggest and most important backer of Biafra and its support for the rebel state was considerable. Its involvement in oil extraction in that region was substantial with a significant operation in Gabon as well as Nigeria itself. It has been suggested that France funded its support of Biafra with the profits from its Nigerian oil fields. Furthermore the proximity of Libreville and Port-Gentil to Nige-

A petrol pump symbolising the dependence of the modern world on oil based energy; the supply of which has caused many conflicts.

Source: http://commons.wikimedia.org/wiki/File:Petrol_pump_in_Macroom.jpg

ria made those towns convenient staging posts for flights to Biafra. France was said to regard stability in its former colonies as a most important issue and as it already had established oil interests in Nigeria it is interesting to consider why General De Gaulle supported the instability which the Biafran war represented. Perhaps France was seeking a greater share of Nigerian oil.

In Rhodesia at the time the media were very strong on the issue of how civilians, especially children, were suffering due to the Nigerian strategy of creating a famine in Biafra and this gave some of the employees at Air Trans Africa the feeling that they were supporting the "right" side.

There were also other countries involved in this brutal war which supported one side or the other.

The years of the Biafran War coincided with the height of the Cold War and especially with the American mismanagement of its war in Vietnam. Both sides of the protracted international stand-off we call the Cold War were prepared to interfere in conflict areas around the world in which they perceived some geo-political advantage might accrue to them. Without the interference of the "great powers" the Biafran War would not have amounted to anywhere near as much hardship for the people involved. Fighting for one's freedom is certainly honourable but it sometimes comes at an enormous cost and the freedom sought may not necessarily be achieved. It takes great wisdom to know when to fight and when to put up. Biafran losses, especially civilian losses were truly terrible.

When this war broke out in Nigeria Jack Malloch was well placed to supply transport to the Biafrans.

A Rhodesian entrepreneur

In the face of all the challenges facing him back home in Salisbury Jack Malloch needed some extra-special entrepreneurial skills and the question was now where would his next charter flights come from?

In January 1967 Jack got into his DC-4 and headed North in search of business. Although by this time Nigeria society was already in serious trouble with a major coup and a substantial amount of serious civil unrest, the civil war was still some months away.

A few weeks later I drove my ancient Austin Cambridge south and headed back to university to complete my economics and political science degree. I had no idea at this stage whether Air Trans Africa would survive the next few months and I did not suspect for a moment that I would work for the company during all my subsequent university vacations and that Jack would offer me a permanent job after I finished my degree.

If anyone in Air Trans Africa knew where Jack was heading then the conspiracy of silence was working really well. It is more likely that no one knew and maybe Jack himself wasn't sure where his travel would take him before he found the work he was looking for.

There isn't much written or for that matter said about how Air Trans Africa survived this period. Money started to come into the Air Trans Africa bank account. Some of it was transferred by Jack from his Swiss account, some was paid directly into the Air Trans Africa bank account and some was brought home by Jack. No one knew how much money Jack had in Switzerland and who his ultimate backers were during this period could only be a matter of mere guess work. It is fairly safe to say that Jack had some resources behind him but I suspect that they were not great and at this time it was urgent for him to find new business.

However on one occasion in the second half of 1967 when I was working for Jack he came into the office I shared with Bob Nesbit and handed Bob a large cardboard box. "Please do count the money and then lock up the box", said Jack. "There was originally two hundred thousand US dollars here but I had to spend some of it on expenses".

In the event there was very nearly the two hundred thousand US dollars in that plain cardboard box in small notes. Bob who before I arrived at the company had virtually no knowledge of accounting and hardly ever handled money became a first class cashier for the company. He used to enjoy very much taking thirty or forty thousand dollars into the bank where the manager had been especially mean to him a few weeks before and having this money converted into local currency and lodged into the account of Air Trans Africa.

Where Jack went in the early months of 1967 is a matter of speculation. It is said that he flew in various troubled zones in Africa and even in the Near East. The code of silence held and thus it is not clear exactly where he was and it doesn't really matter. He was earning money and the company was recovering. However by the outbreak of the Biafra War he was well established as an important air carrier in that conflict. I have seen Jack described as a gun runner but I am not aware of his ever buying or selling weapons or ammunition. He did not make money out of buying and selling his cargo. Jack was in fact an aircraft operator who was prepared to fly in and out of and within war zones. He hired out the capacity of his airplanes. I have also seen Jack described as a mercenary which I guess in the broadest sense of the word he was. But the term mercenary has a strongly negative connotation and the other mercenaries I met in South Africa who fought with Mike Hoare seemed to like the idea of fighting. I did not ever obtain this type of feeling from Jack Malloch. Jack was flying in and out of war zones because that was where he could find work for his aircraft and their crews. For me this was simply the extreme end of entrepreneurship. As soon as he was able to Jack ceased this type of work and returned to flying regular commercial routes.

The code of silence in Air Trans Africa was so strong that we knew very little about the routes that the aircraft took and the payloads which they carried during the Biafran period. The work was obviously very dangerous because the crews earned breathtaking sums of money. They would be paid per flight and it was rumoured that generally they made a flight every night and each flight earned the crew considerably more than their monthly salary. The fee was paid to them directly in cash. After the fall of Port Harcourt to the Federal forces, Jack's flights were mostly to Uli, which was an airstrip created out of an enlarged country road. There was no formal air traffic control and the landing lights were the headlights of parked motor vehicles. The lights on the ground and on the aircraft were kept to a minimum as there was always the fear that the Nigerian Air Force was close by and would see and thus be able to shoot down the supply airplanes. It is hard to overstate just how dangerous it was to fly under these conditions and it is actually surprising that there were so few incidents.

The pay for this type of flying was very good and some of this new found wealth which came to Jack's staff was reflected in the appearance of new cars and new houses etc. In addition all the back pay which was owed was paid and thus there was a general atmosphere of opulence among the air crew. Although the office staff did not share much in this new wealth there was no obvious resentment in this respect.

We did know that ordinance was involved and we also knew that Air Trans Africa flew children out of Biafra. There are now accounts on the web of aircraft taking in guns one night and powdered milk the next. I would have expected Jack to top up his planes with food and medical supplies if he had capacity and if these types of supplies were to hand. We actually were very poorly informed about the general course of the war but we did know that one of the military strategies of the Nigerian Government was to create a famine in the breakaway territory. The Nigerians were clear that this was a perfectly acceptable approach to warfare and they made no allowances for the fact that this had a particularly hard impact on women and children. Heart wrenching photos of babies and toddlers on the point of death from starvation were published in the press and aired on television.

We knew that the planes flew from various Portuguese territories to a few different sites in Biafra. There were also regular visits to Gabon where the crews took short breaks. The crews came home to Salisbury every few weeks for a reasonable period of R&R but the money they were making meant that they wanted to get as many trips as they could.

In between his operational flying Jack would have to go to Paris for financial and strategy meetings. On one occasion Bob and Iris Nesbit accompanied him and on another occasion I joined Jack in Paris.

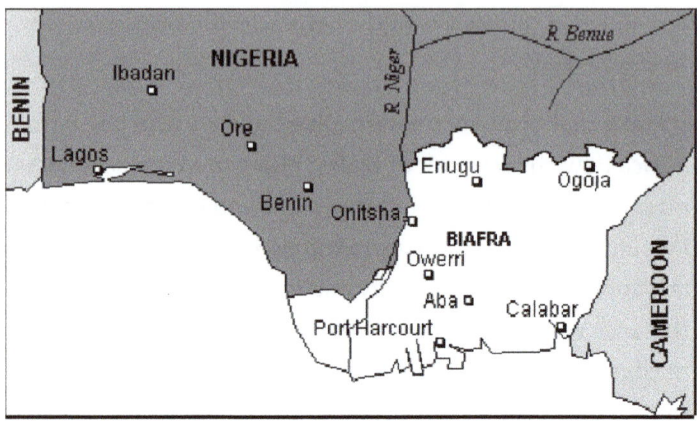

The Republic of Biafra was constituted from the South Eastern province of Nigeria. As can be seen from this map it was a small part of the whole country.
Source:http://commons.wikimedia.org/wiki/File:Biafra_independent_state_map-en.svg

In all Jack was not often seen in Salisbury and this was not good for the company especially as he was not prepared to appoint a deputy in his absence. Jack took the view that if everyone did their job then the company would function well and that matters requiring his attention could wait until he came home, which I guess was generally about once a month.

The DC-7F was regarded as a more reliable aircraft than the DC-7Cs which Jack had used for his passenger charter service a few years before.
Source:http://commons.wikimedia.org/wiki/File:Aer_Turas_Douglas_DC-7B(F)_Wheatley.jpg

Jack's fleet had expanded and during this period he acquired several DC-7Fs. These were dedicated air freighters and were to become the backbone of Air Trans Africa's post-Biafran operation.

One of the things we did not know about was the scale of the airlift into Biafra. Of course we knew that Jack was not the only operator but it came as a great surprise when we read years later that the Biafran airlift was the second largest in the history of aviation, only being superseded by the Berlin Airlift. Most of the aircraft in this endeavour only flew food and medical supplies and were organised by aid agencies and church charities. Jack was not one of these relief operators as he mostly carried ordinance.

It might be said that the Nigerian Government tolerated the humanitarian airlift in that they did not as actively shoot them down as perhaps they could have but they openly threatened the ordinance air carriers whom they saw as the enemy.

It has been estimated that at its peak in 1969, the airlift delivered an average of 250 metric tons of food each night to the estimated 2 million people dependent on these supplies. About 20 flights were flown each night and this made the makeshift airstrip at Uli one of the busiest runways in Africa. Despite this effort they were only able to carry about 10% of the amount of food actually needed. It is said that over 5,300 missions were flown by ten different carriers, and that 60,000 tons of humanitarian aid was delivered. As mentioned earlier about three million civilians died in this war, many from starvation. In addition it has been estimated that about 30 air crew died either from accidents or from the actions of the Nigerian Forces.

What happens in war!
The money paid to the Air Trans Africa crew for flying in a war zone was generally well earned. The Nigerian Air Force operated MIG

fighters that were said to be flown by Egyptian pilots. As already mentioned much of the flying had to be done in the dark so that the possibility of collision was greatly enhanced. There were many near misses but very few tragedies.

Jack lost one aircraft which was his DC-4. It was said at the time that the pilot lost his orientation and pointed the aircraft in the wrong direction before takeoff. However this has not been confirmed. Remembering that there were no runway lights and that the aircraft lights themselves had to be switched off it appears that the pilot could not see in which direction he was heading. Only one of Jack's fulltime crew members was killed in the whole Biafran operation.

A DC-4 similar to the one that Jack had and which crashed on takeoff in Biafra.

Source:http://commons.wikimedia.org/wiki/File:Douglas_DC-4_Flying_Dutchman.jpg

On a subsequent occasion another crew member had a close shave with death when his appendix burst on takeoff from Biafra on the way to Lisbon. In the old Super Connie the flight time was about 10 hours depending on head winds etc. This was considered too long and therefore an emergency stop was made in Guinea Bissau. A ruptured appendix can be fatal and surgery was immediately required. It appears that they were just in time to save the life of this pilot. Of course the flight couldn't wait to see what the outcome of the operation was. The pilot was hospitalised for over a month and took several additional weeks to find his way back to Salisbury.

Perhaps the most striking incident in this Biafran period occurred to Jack himself together with three other members of crew. When Biafra broke away from Nigeria the Biafran Government took possession of a substantial amount of Nigerian currency in the form of bank notes. These bank notes were then used by the Biafrans to fund the purchase of war materials. The Nigerians decided to put an end to this by withdrawing this currency from use and issuing new Nigerian bank notes. This they did in a relatively short period of time, at the end of which all previous Nigerian bank notes were to become null and void. This was a major operation and the Biafrans clearly did not realise that their opponents in Lagos were able to pull this trick off in such a short time frame. January 22 1968 was set as the date that the old Nigerian money would no longer be legal tender. Due to the general confusion of these times the Biafran government were not able to produce their own currency by the time the Nigerian money was withdrawn and this led to another level of difficulty which the new Republic had to face.

So at the beginning of January the Biafrans had a substantial amount of Nigerian bank notes which they needed to place in the international market as quickly as possible. A plan was made whereby Jack and another air carrier working for the Biafrans would fly the bank notes to Switzerland and lodge them into the Biafrans' Swiss bank account. This would effectively be converting Nigerian pounds to Swiss Francs which would then be used to continue to fund the war.

A Nigerian bank note, typical of those carried by Jack.

Source: Private collection of Dan Remenyi

On January 12 two aircraft left Biafra with about 20 tons of Nigerian bank notes. At this stage the value of a Nigerian pound which had been on par with a pound sterling had lost 40% and was now only 12 shillings to the pound. One of these planes was flown by Jack who was carrying approximately 13 tons of paper money. On arrival in Switzerland Jack was refused entry as he was travelling on a Rhodesian registered aircraft and Switzerland had no diplomatic relations with the former British colony. The Swiss refused to unload the cargo and the aircraft was forced to leave. Jack flew to Lisbon where he knew he would be allowed to land. However the Portuguese banks could not accept this amount of Nigerian money. With the exchange rate dropping rapidly every day and only a week left before the 13 tons of paper money would become valueless there was intense pressure to find a way of processing this money into the international banking system so that it could be repatriated to Nigeria in order to obtain value from it. There had been in the previous months a considerable amount of smuggling of relatively small sums of Nigerian money out of Biafra and then re-smuggled back into Nigeria to be deposited with the Lagos banks and be available to be withdrawn when the new Nigerian bank notes were issued. Now the plan was to do the same but on a much larger scale.

It took some days to decide how this should be done. Finally a plan was established that Jack would fly to Lomé in Togo with the 13 tons of money on board. Jack was to be met there by a friendly official who would receive the money and who was in a position to have it transported the 500 kilometres out of Lomé through Benin and on to Lagos where it would be lodged in a bank which was friendly to the Biafran cause. Togo had been a French colony and Jack believed that he had good connections in the government in that country to make him feel that such arrangements could be made and that promises would be fulfilled. He was equipped with the names of the appropriate people and told how they were to be approached.

Unfortunately on arrival in Lomé the contact man with which Jack was to work was nowhere to be seen. His networking with his French colleagues had failed to deliver the friendly Togo face Jack was expecting to meet. As a result Jack and the crew were detained, the money was confiscated and the aircraft was left standing on the runway where its remains are said to still rest today. Lomé is six degrees north of the equator and it would not have taken long, perhaps only months, for the aircraft to have rotted to the extent that it would never fly again. But it is said that the Togolese actually bulldozed the aircraft and thus permanently wrecked it.

Back in Salisbury we had heard that Jack had flown to Switzerland and that he had been refused entry due to the aircraft being Rhodesian registered. We knew that he had then taken the cargo to Lisbon and we were all quite anxious as to whether he would be able to find a solution to this problem before the money became valueless.

> There are numerous rumours about what actually happened in Togoland. Bob Nisbet was of the view that the French connection which Jack had did a very sloppy job in making the arrangements to off load the Nigerian money. It clearly did not matter much to them, the French if the money arrived at the bank in time.
>
> There was a rumour that Jack was stopped at the airport in Lomé because one of his crew had a hidden gun on his person. It will never be possible to know if this was true and if it were then how important it might have been as a cause for their arrest.
>
> Initially we were given the impression that Jack and his crew were treated well by the Togolese, but subsequently we heard that this was not the case and that at one time Jack was marched at gun point down the main street of Lomé in his underwear.
>
> There was no suggestion that the crew were made to engage in hard labour. It was said that they went through many packets of playing cards.
>
> I spoke to an eye witness who went to Lomé as part of the group seeking Jack's release. The only information I obtained was that the legal proceedings were held in a wood and iron building not at all like the buildings Rhodesians were accustomed to for law courts. Nonetheless the Togolese lawyers wore the black gowns and wigs of their profession.

But we did not hear about Lomé in advance. It is not difficult to imagine that the office was completely stunned by this news of Jack's detention. How was Air Trans Africa going to function without Jack at the helm?

Somehow it did. Bob Nesbit hunkered down Air Trans Africa and awaited the return of Jack.

These were dark days indeed for Jack. It appears that more than once he was threatened with the death penalty – execution by firing squad - although he was probably worth much more to the Togo government alive than dead. It was not ever made clear what sort of charges were levelled against him, if any. From a Nigerian point of view Jack was carrying stolen money, albeit on behalf of the Biafrans. Togo was an independent francophone country and didn't need to take the Nigerian point of view too seriously. At one point it was suggested that if a large payment was made Jack, the crew and the aircraft would be released but this was opposed as it was tantamount to paying a ransom.

After about five months and paying a fine Jack and his crew were released and he returned to Lisbon and picked up the reigns of the company exactly where he had left off. However with little income and lots of company expenses for the previous five months Jack was back in a financial quagmire again. Fortunately the high earnings from the Biafra flights allowed Air Trans Africa to financially recover fairly quickly.

Incidentally Jack was a man who was slightly overweight by as much as a half or even one stone. When he returned from Lomé he was that much under weight. In keeping with the code of silence very little was said about his time in detention except that the Togolese appear to have been convinced, at least originally, that Jack had stolen the money for himself and that was one of their main motives for detaining him. It is more likely that he was a pawn in a political power game in West Africa which had to play itself out. By now Biafra had its own money and that was printed in Europe and had to be flown out to Africa. This Biafran money was not of any real value to anyone outside of that country which was well on its way to losing the war. Nonetheless it was to cause trouble for Jack. On arriving at the office one morning I saw a police car in the company car park and I was greeted by Bob Nesbit who was wearing a very down-in-the-dumps expression. "What is the matter?" I asked. "A lot of money has been stolen," he said. I immediately thought that someone had been able to break into the safe but fortunately this was not the case. "It appears," said Bob, "some members of the crew have brought back a few rucksacks of Biafran money without telling anybody that they were taking it." "What would they do that for?" I asked incredulously. "I guess souvenirs. What else could it be for?" said Bob. "And the trouble is that the Biafran government is holding Jack personally responsible for this." "What does that actually mean?" I asked feeling more like Alice in Wonderland with every second that went by. "We could lose our Biafran work!" was the sombre reply.

A Biafran bank note, similar to those that went missing in Salisbury. No mention was ever made of the denominations of these bank notes but they were of no value.

Source: Private collection of Dan Remenyi

Officers of the BSAP spoke to a number of people. Phone calls were made by Air Trans Africa staff to all the members of the crew who were in the country as a deep depression set in on the company. It looked like no one at Air Trans Africa had a clue who had taken the money and it seemed such a ridiculous thing to have done as it would have no value at all outside of Biafra. However the word did get around to whoever was involved and the issue was taken very seriously. Late that night the police received an anonymous phone call to say that they would find something of special interest in one of the storm drains at a cross road in the centre of Salisbury. How the police handled this type of call was not revealed to us but we were told that when they investigated, a couple of rucksacks stuffed with Biafran money were retrieved and returned to Jack who personally carried them back with appropriate apologies to Biafra.

The Biafran cash cow for Jack was not over yet and would not be for some time.

Back in Salisbury

So the regular flow of money into the business again meant that normality was restored to the operations of Air Trans Africa as a commercial concern back at Salisbury Airport. The company had been put back onto a sound financial footing and was paying its way in the manner that would have been expected of any properly run business. The financial reserves were in good shape. Jack had acquired several DC-7 Fs and had expanded the number of aircrew who were now a much more international group.

Jack was now looking for other commercial opportunities in Salisbury. One such opportunity was a small air freight clearing business which he bought and which I was offered to manage. It ran well for a year but the effect of sanctions began to be felt. It was going to need a lot of time, energy and money to make it a success if that could be done at all under the circumstances of growing sanctions and Jack had other things in mind.

Jack began to mention that he was on the lookout for a jet airplane. When I first heard this I wondered how a small company such as Air Trans Africa would be able to afford to move into this new technological area. Not only would the purchase of a jet aircraft cost much more that the company could afford but the infrastructure required to support such a piece of equipment as well as the new or retrained crews could cost millions. Bob Nesbit was adamant. "If Jack has even mentioned a jet, that means that he has already started to make arrangements to acquire one. Expect a jet to be parked outside the hangar here soon." It did take a year but the jet arrived.

The Air Trans Africa hangar in Salisbury showing the 3 DC-7s and the Super Connie sporting the Afro-Continental Airways name which was used for a short time by Jack.

Source: McGeorge Photography, Zimbabwe

Jack was also on the lookout for business opportunities with Gabon and he realised that Air Trans Africa may now have become too associated with his Biafra operation to be acceptable to normal Gabonese or European business interests. He therefore floated a new company which he called Afro-Continental Airways Limited. This would be the new corporate vehicle with which he would acquire a jet freighter and return to normal commercial operations.

One of Jack's initiatives during this period was to establish a scheduled air service between Salisbury and Windhoek. There was a once a week service between these two cities. There was no obvious reason why there should be adequate traffic between these locations and within a month or so the experimental service had to be abandoned. This brief episode does show Jack's interest in wanting to establish himself as a regular commercial airline operator. From a Rhodesian point of view this was flying the flag and showing that the country had the resources to offer such a service.

This Windhoek experiment which was wasteful of national resources was indicative of the fact that Jack had not yet obtained the support from the Rhodesian government and that he was not at that stage seen as a serious air transport player who had an important role to play alongside the National Carrier. Air Rhodesia was still playing the role of the dog in the manger.

In the early days of sanctions Rhodesians generally felt that these measures were going to be a damp squid. Nearly everyone in Salisbury laughed at Wilson for the comment about how sanctions would bring Rhodesia to its knees *in months if not weeks*. Rhodesia had a strong economy with a favourable balance of payments and a good rate of growth. It had a strong technological base with transportation and communications links. It had a relatively highly educated population of both white and black people. Many of the organisations which traded with Rhodesian companies were reluctant to give up their profitable relationships. However being out of the sterling area meant that Rhodesians experienced difficulties with foreign exchange. This was initially felt by the white population, many of whom had families in South Africa and overseas, through the reduction in the travel allowance which was curtailed at £50 per person per year. This made foreign travel very difficult. Shortly after this petrol rationing was introduced by the issuing of ration coupons. Thus the availability of petrol was very tight although there was some saving up of petrol coupons and borrowing and lending of them amongst friends. Going for a drive in the country had to be carefully thought about in order not to run out of fuel before the end of the week. Then there were a number of commodities which could previously be purchased and now disappeared from the market. Generally these were luxury items and were only missed by the more well to do in the mink and manure set.

Rhodesian industry responded well to finding ways and means of producing local substitutes and these actually gave a direct boost to the economy. However some of these locally produced goods were inferior in comparison to the originals and the one which comes immediately to mind was the locally produced whisky. The tobacco growing industry changed its modus operandi by reducing prices and ensuring secrecy to any organisations which purchased their crop.

Although there was no serious inflation during this period many items did experience small increases in prices as Rhodesian importers often had to use middle men in order to disguise the fact that certain goods were actually bound for consumption in Rhodesia.

Of course not everyone supported the Rhodesian Front and the declaration of independence but the majority of white voters did. The Rhodesian Front took all the white seats in the parliament. Some of these who did not support Ian Smith took the view that it was time to leave and they sold their goods and chattels and emigrated. Mostly these people moved south but some went back to Great Britain or Europe. It was not uncommon to see a motor vehicle, sometimes with a trailer attached, on its way to Beitbridge which was the main border post with South Africa. These emigrants could only take some of their used household goods and £50 each in cash. This lack of money trapped many people who would like to have left but could not envisage a life outside of Rhodesia with so little funds.

It is often said that the first victim of a war is freedom of expression and thus the Smith Government became very sensitive to any criticism and the media came under tight control. The Rhodesian Herald was placed under direct censorship and all material printed in that newspaper had to be inspected before it went to press. Whenever the censors refused to allow an article to be printed the newspaper left a blank or white space on the page. Thus it was usually known when something was happening that the government did not want the public to know about. Of course this led to lots of random guessing which was not always helpful.

From this photo it may be hard to believe that there could be long delays in passing through the immigration and custom formalities at Beitbridge.
Source:http://commons.wikimedia.org/wlkl/File:Beitbridge_borderpost.jpg

Despite these inconveniences the general atmosphere in Rhodesia at this time among the whites was relatively positive. These people wanted to believe in Ian Smith and his prediction that there would not be majority rule in his lifetime. However war was inevitable and was Rhodesia equipped to take on a major conflict? The answer to this was clearly *No*, but the ensuing conflict started slowly and took a number of years before it became a major part of everyone's life in Rhodesia.

The building of Affretair

At its height Air Trans Africa or Affretair as it became known by the end of the 1970s employed about 200 full time staff and maybe another couple of hundred temporary, part-timers. The company was flying up to eight return flights a week to Europe. It would have been carrying about 1000 tons of fresh produce per month mainly beef and returning to Salisbury with items which could not otherwise have been easily acquired. Jack is on record as saying that he did not carry ordinance at this stage. He stated that many of the people and organisations with whom he worked and who were prepared to ignore sanctions would have walked away from him if it were to be shown that he was carrying military equipment.

Although this transformation is clearly credited to Jack it is pretty obvious that he did not do all the painstaking work which was required to move the fledgling Air Trans Africa of the mid 1960s into the organisation it became by the mid-1970s. Jack was an ideas man with the energy and the nouse to make things happen. He was not, however, a detailed administrator. Of course, in general managing directors don't do all the hard work. To have a successful organisation the managing director has to be able to attract the right people around him and keep them all committed to the vision of the enterprise. This Jack did splendidly. He found and he brought into the company the right people. Jack's leadership qualities made this whole thing work and when he had gone it quickly fell to pieces.

A 1000 tons of fresh produce a month is a staggering amount for the small operation which was Affretair. The frequency of flights and the cargo volumes carried meant that the organisation had to operate at a high degree of efficiency and at a suitable level of profitability. Close coordination with the Cold Storage Commission was essential. The documentation which accompanied these exports had to be produced in such a way that they were acceptable to the countries to which the goods were destined as well as being opaque to those who were monitoring the enforcement of sanctions.

Jack had built a new hangar and a new office complex. In operating the DC-8s he had acquired additional crew with a completely different set of flying and engineering skills. His home base engineering operation had to be completely revamped. In the old days i.e. the 1960s, Jack's engineering operation had been described by some as being akin to Steptoe and Son's business, but it had been completely restructured and became highly regarded in the industry in Rhodesia. This required a substantial investment and a considerable amount of technical and management skill.

At this level of operation air crew training becomes a major consideration and Jack found it necessary to create the structures required to ensure that everyone was kept fully up to international levels in this respect.

All of this was achieved during increasing pressure from sanctions and a deteriorating situation as regards the Bush War. Creating such an international air freight carrier as Affretair is certainly a tribute to Jack Malloch's leadership and management skills.

With Affretair's success Jack began to be perceived in Salisbury as less of a maverick and he increasingly became part of the business establishment in Rhodesia. This was reinforced by the role he played in supporting military operations in the country. He was offered a commission in the Rhodesian Air Force Volunteer Reserve.

Eventually Affretair was recognised as being the National Freight Carrier for Rhodesia. Jack's ambition was now to expand the company and make it one of the leading airfreight businesses in Africa with an even greater reach than it had at that time.

The Bush War or Chimurenga

Insurgencies often start on a very small scale and the violence creeps up quite slowly on the defenders until they eventually find themselves involved in what has become a large scale conflict or war. It is also often the case that the defenders cannot envision how they could possibly lose until the enemy is truly at the gate and even then some people want to fight on no matter how impossible the situation is. And so it was in Rhodesia.

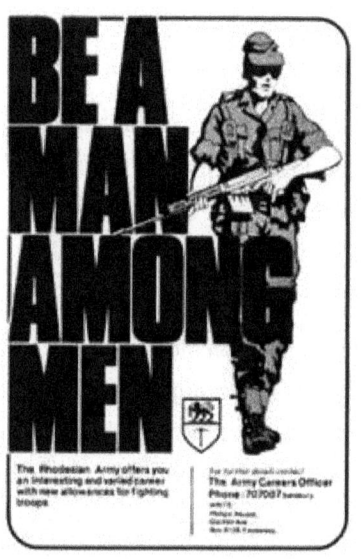

The Rhodesian Bush war is reckoned by some to have begun in July 1964 with an incident in which a white man was killed, and by this reckoning the war was to last 15 years and to cost about 20,000 lives. But the first major engagement took place in April 1966 when seven ZANLA (Zimbabwe African National Liberation Army) men were killed. In return for this the ZANLA survivors of this encounter with the Rhodesian security forces killed two farmers at rural Hartley a short while later. There were two major factions within the guerrilla movement. Firstly, there was Mugabe's ZANLA backed by China and then there was Nkomo's ZIPRA (Zimbabwe People's Revolutionary Army) backed by the Soviet Union.

This sort of insurgent activity in the 1960s was not considered a major threat to the state. There was an astonishing naivety about the capability of the opponents of the Smith government. It was commonly held that black people had no facility with technology and therefore would be hopeless with modern armaments. It was claimed that if black people were given explosives they would blow themselves up before they could do any harm to the security forces. In the light of the events which were going on in Africa at this time it is hard to understand how these paternalistic prejudices could exist at all. But they did and people who seemed to be intelligent believed them. I guess this was part of the self-delusions which were common even among politicians and were clearly demonstrated by both Ian Smith and Harold Wilson. When some years later the Viscounts were blown out of the sky the national shock was palpable. There is no doubt that the guerrillas had some catching up to do but they had a lot of resources on their side both in terms of fighters and also in terms of big powerful partners which were interested in using Rhodesia as a pawn in the Cold War and thus wanted to see the Smith government fall. To the Soviet Union and China Rhodesia was not only a racist regime but a capitalist state that they would have been delighted to have been able to claim they had contributed to bringing down.

It is important to note that in these early years of the liberation struggle the rural population of Rhodesia was nowhere near as politicised as they were to eventually become. Smith was probably right when he declared that the local people were suspicious of the African nationalists, preferring their own tribal leadership structures, and were not that much discontented with the status quo. However that was to radically change in the ensuring years.

By the end of the 1960s Smith had arranged for support from South Africa to patrol the border with Zambia and South African police were sent north for this purpose. They remained part of Rhodesia's northern border defence until the mid-1970s. It is interesting to ask why South Africa supplied police for this purpose. It has been suggested that the South Africans perceived the guerrillas as being criminal elements who were entering Rhodesia more as vandals than for political purposes. If this was truly the case then it could be considered another example of self-delusion. In any event their motivation hardly matters and the South African police were a paramilitary organisation so they fitted in with the Rhodesian military. Some Rhodesians suggested that South Africa only sent these men north so that they would obtain counter insurgency experience to be used back home in the fullness of time.

Although the guerrilla activity had increased substantially by the early 1970s it was still thought to be controllable especially as long as the Portuguese and the South Africans were on side. It was clearly in South Africa's and Portugal's interests to have a white controlled Rhodesia if for no other reason than it meant that there was one less border to worry about, but at this time the political sands were drifting or shifting dramatically in Africa as well as in other parts of the world. By the early 1970s the Americans were in deep trouble in Vietnam and the lessons which were to be ultimately learnt from that conflict had not yet been fully appreciated and certainly had not been picked up by the Rhodesians.

Ultimately the problem for Smith was that neither South Africa nor Portugal would remain on his side for long and Rhodesia on its own could not resist the insurgents trained and equipped by the Soviet Union and China. In the early days the nationalists operated from secluded bases in Zambia and from a small number of remote FRELIMO (Frente de Libertação de Moçambique or in English the Mozambique Liberation Front) controlled areas of Mozambique but with the collapse of the Salazar regime in Portugal, the Mozambique situation changed.

An Air Rhodesia viscount, two of which were shot down by the insurgents.
Source:http://commons.wikimedia.org/wiki/File:Air_Rhodesia_Vickers_748D_Viscount_Wheatley.jpg

António de Oliveira Salazar was Prime Minister of Portugal from 1932 to 1968. He ran the country as a virtual dictator. He was a conservative, a nationalist and an anti-communist. He was intent on keeping the Portuguese Empire intact despite the winds of change which the other empires were experiencing. Although Portugal had a number of colonies around the world it had not been a real world power for many years. The South American countries had won their independence from Spain and Portugal in the early part of the 19th century with Portugal's army surrendering to the Brazilian rebels in 1824 and Portugal granting independence in 1825. Nonetheless Portugal had a material presence in Africa.

Salazar was said to have been a personal friend of Ian Smith and that fact has been offered in part as an account for Portugal's support for the Rhodesian Government. But this is nonsense. Having a white pro-Portugal government in Rhodesia meant that the Portuguese troops fighting their own insurgents in Mozambique did not have to be overly concerned with guerrillas infiltrating their territory from the West. Collaboration between Rhodesia and the Portuguese Empire was of mutual and immediate benefit.

Desfile do 10 de Junho na Marginal de Luanda

The Portuguese were in no hurry to give up their Empire.

Source:http://commons.wikimedia.org/wiki/File:Desfiledo10deJunhonamarginalde Luanda.jpg

Although Salazar himself died in 1970 his successors continued with his regime including the colonial wars in Africa and there was considerable relief in Rhodesia that there would be business as usual with Portugal. But those who were interested in regional politics knew that the cost of the Portuguese colonial wars was enormous especially for a small relatively poor country and that major changes were inevitable.

In April 1974, the left-wing Carnation Revolution in Portugal heralded the end of the Portuguese Empire and colonial rule in Mozambique. On June 25, 1975 when it was obvious that Portugal could no longer sustain the loss of life and treasure, Mozambique became an independent country controlled by FRELIMO who gave their support to anti-Smith guerrillas and thus added another 800 miles of hostile border to the country. Up to this point it could be argued that Rhodesia was able to hold its own in the Bush War but now the tide had turned against the former colony.

Inspecting an Allouette helicopter of the type used by Fireforce in the Bush War.

Source: Private collection of Paul Dubois.

It was at this time that the Rhodesian military created the Fireforce initiative in which Jack played a role. Fireforce has been described as a military tactic of attacking a guerrilla target by helicopter-borne and parachuted infantry. It involved the early identification of guerrillas and then rushing to engage them before they could damage Rhodesian targets. Fireforce was essentially an airborne facilitated strategy which required both helicopters as well as fixed wing aircraft to carry more troops than the helicopters could as well as additional supplies.

Clearly Jack was a major asset to the air force in this respect and he was able to support the Rhodesian forces both within Rhodesia and when necessary in the former Portuguese colony of Mozambique. It has also been said that when the Air Force needed any long-range transports it borrowed the appropriate aircraft from Air Trans Africa whose owner, Jack Malloch, was an officer in the Volunteer Reserve.

By the way, when Portugal withdrew from Africa in 1976 a million Portuguese living in their former colonies were displaced and most had to return to Portugal. Some moved to Rhodesia and South Africa. The vacuum left behind by Portugal triggered a civil war in Mozambique which lasted until 1982 when a peace accord was reached.

Although Mozambique closed its border, Rhodesian forces crossed the border in "hot pursuit" raids, attacking the nationalists and their training camps. More and more men were needed by the Rhodesian army and the duration of army service was extended to a wider range of ages and to a regime of six weeks in and six weeks out of uniform. The situation was now much more difficult with the Rhodesian military informing the government that they could no longer stem the flood of guerrillas into the country and it became clear that some political settlement with black leaders would be needed.

Following an ambush on the road from Fort Victoria to Beitbridge in 1976 all road traffic on this route was restricted to convoy which were often escorted by a number of armoured Land Rovers. The convoy was lead by two of these vehicles and the rear was protected by another two, while two other Land Rovers moved up and down the convoy. Up to 150 vehicles travelled in this way between the two towns often taking about three and a half hours for the trip during which no comfort break were permitted. Although the Fort Victoria to Beitbridge route was the first to use the convoy ap-

A group preparing to set off on a convoy. From their dress it is winter in the Eastern Highlands.
Source: Private collection

proach it eventually became necessary to use convoys for traffic between other cities.

The emigration numbers from Rhodesia began to climb and the delays at Beit Bridge increased.

The Bush War had moved into its end game now with an imminent Rhodesian defeat becoming a real possibility. The first passenger aircraft to be lost in the war, a viscount called *Hunyani*, was Air Rhodesia Flight 825 on September 3, 1978 short down shortly after takeoff from Kariba Airport. The second, Flight 827 was another Air Rhodesia viscount called *Umniati* downed on February 12, 1979, also at Kariba. There were survivors from the first aircraft but they were subsequently killed by guerrillas on the ground. By this stage white Rhodesians had their opinions changed for them by their experience of black fighters whose ability to handle the technology of war was becoming more and more obvious. In fact before the war was over the Rhodesian Army had recruited many black soldiers for their side and these played an important role especially in the Selous Scouts.

To many people's amazement the Smith government still saw their continuance in power in some form as viable and they believed that they would be able to largely dictate the type and manner of the political settlement within the country and they began a dialogue with Bishop Able Muzorewa. This was another act of self delusion as the Bishop could only be seen as a Smith puppet. However time was running out for Smith and it was clear that the game was up when South Africa which had been encouraging Smith to reach a settlement with black leaders for some time, decided that it was no longer in their interest to continue supporting the rebel Rhodesia. It was now a question of how to cease hostilities and how to transform the country.

A question which is sometimes asked is *What was the cost of a war?* And sometimes this is answered in terms of money and in terms of lives lost. Of course, it is never possible to give an accurate account of the casualties of a war. But the published figures suggest that in the Rhodesia Bush War 1361 members of the Security Forces and 10,000 guerrillas were killed as well as 468 white civilians and 7790 black civilians. This would be nearly 20,000 people. However other sources suggest that the number was nearer 30,000 people. Of course the actual numbers will never be known.

Kissinger pulls the plug?

In June 1976 the American Secretary of State met with the South African Prime Minister in West-Germany to discuss Rhodesia. Henry Kissinger explained to John Vorster that the United States of America could no longer remain indifferent about the affairs of Southern Africa and that they wanted to see the end of the rebel regime in Rhodesia. There was more internal trouble in Angola and Mozambique where the cold war was playing itself out in not such a "cold" fashion. Communist victories across Africa from Angola, through Rhodesia to Mozambique would be disastrous for the United States which had been severely humiliated by the victory of the Communist backed Viet Cong in South East Asia. Any other Communist victories in military conflict situations would have further impacted on

America's dwindling prestige even if the American military itself was not directly involved.

Kissinger was instrumental in changing regimes in various parts of the world.
Source:http://commons.wikimedia.org/wiki/File:Reuni%C3%B3n_Pinochet_-_Kissinger.jpg?uselang=en-gb

Kissinger pointed out that it was now in South Africa's urgent interest to help bring the Bush War in Rhodesia to an end and thus expedite the transfer of government of that country to majority rule. South Africa could do this with a stroke of a pen as Rhodesia was now dependent on South Africa for petroleum, electric power, water and many other commodities. The deal proposed by Kissinger was that majority rule was to be put into place in Rhodesia within two years.

Because of this role in bringing the Rhodesian rebellion to an end Kissinger is described on some websites as the second most evil man who ever lived. The suggestion is that he wanted to destroy white Christian civilisation in Africa and that he had a personal responsibility for what happened. It is hard to believe that he was anything more than the instrument of American government policy which had little concern for what was happening in Africa except that it did not want to see any progress made by those receiving support from Soviet Union, China, Cuba or North Korea. Africa has never been of central importance to America and it is not clear to me that Kissinger personally deserves any real credit or blame for what happened.

Kissinger's intervention was not wholly unwelcome in Salisbury where some of the important members of the Smith Government understood that it was better to be perceived as having been betrayed by the American and the South Africans and thus forced by them to peace talks than having to either surrender to the insurgents or suffer a defeat in the field. Nonetheless there were still those who wanted an Alamo type end to the Republic of Rhodesia.

It is interesting to reflect on the South African role in the Bush War as they had been prepared to give some help to Smith and as mentioned before had even supplied police to assist patrolling the border with Zambia but they did not see their interests as being identical with the Rhodesians. After all many of the Rhodesians were settlers, a large number from Great Britain and not white Africans like the Afrikaners. It was convenient for South Africa to have a white controlled neighbour to the North but they did not see this as essential to their security. The Rhodesians and the Afrikaners were not kith and kin. In fact many of those who had helped in the creation of Rhodesia in the early years of the 20th century were the same people who had been implicated in the instigation of the Second Anglo-Boer War which had been brutal for Afrikaner civilians. The South Africans were prepared to do business with any government which might come to power in Rhodesia.

Furthermore the South Africans had been engaged in what might be now considered as a charm offensive in other parts of Africa. They had decided to actively engage with African countries wherever possible in an attempt to be friendly neighbours and this they referred to as their policy of detente. The purpose of this was to deflect some of the criticism of their internal apartheid policies. After all apartheid was a neo-colonial exercise. By this time the ANC's Umkhonto we Sizwe was already well formed and the Soweto riots had already taken place. The clock was already ticking towards South Africa's own transformation to majority rule.

The Angolan civil war had started and South Africa was worried about the presence of Cuban troops. South Africa had sent troops into Angola and had sustained heavy casualties. It has never been admitted how high the casualty rate was but rumour has it that the Cubans inflicted heavy damage on the South African forces.

Thus the South Africans realised that they were in no position to oppose the Americans. They also saw that being part of the Rhodesian solution would be excellent for their image in Africa, as well as the rest of the world, so they were prepared to comply with Kissinger's demands.

Smith himself saw this change in South African policy as a betrayal. The South African intelligence assessment regarding the course of the war was good. Rhodesia was no longer able to hold its own. The resources marshalled against Smith were growing and the insurgents were increasing their tactical skills in the field. South Africa knew that a military victory by the insurgents would bring chaos to its borders. It is thought that contingency plans were made in Pretoria to develop refugee camps in the Northern Transvaal near the Rhodesian border for the possibility of there being a mass exodus of white Rhodesians in the event of there being a military defeat.

It was now a question of which black leaders would take the prize and control the country which would then change its name to Zimbabwe. Smith wanted to minimise the influence of Nkomo or Mugabe but there were others who wanted to fight on in keeping with the spirit of the Alamo. Fortunately this didn't happen and the Lancaster House agreement bringing peace to the country between the Limpopo and the Zambezi, soon to be called Zimbabwe, as well as majority rule was signed on December 21, 1979.

> The effect of the Lancaster House agreement was to replace one ruling elite with another. This was to be expected as it is perhaps the most natural outcome of all revolutions. Countries do not function without ruling elites and the issue is probably only to what extent does the ruling elite have the interests of all the peoples in the country at heart. This of course varies enormously from country to country but in general what is promised in pre-election manifestos is seldom what is actually delivered.

By the way, it is interesting to note that when FW De Klerk was dismantling apartheid some 15 years later and handing South Africa over to the ANC he was asked why the Nationalist Government were giving up their principles of apartheid without a fight. He replied that they decided that they would not hang on like the Rhodesians did and only admit defeat after they had a wrecked and devastated economy and a significantly reduced white population.

Jack and the chilled beef

Back in 1968 and 1969 in the early days of his involvement in Biafra Jack flew empty aircraft from Salisbury to the loading zones for Biafra. This usually involved landing in Libreville in Gabon where the Air Trans Africa crews were in contact with French nationals. The crews began to take with them supplies as Gabon was not known to the

Rhodesians for its culinary choices or for its quality. Rhodesian beef was well known to be one of the best in the world and soon some of the French associates of the company started to request that beef should be brought for them. It didn't take long to realize that Rhodesian beef could be exported this way.

A new company was established in Gabon called Affretair and it became the name of this new corporate vehicle to carry exported Rhodesian beef and other foodstuffs. The existence of this company and the registration of the aircraft in Gabon were facilitated by the trust that had been built up between Jack and his contacts in Paris over the Biafran years.

The final Nigerian offensive against Biafra was launched on January 7, 1970 and shortly after the whole civil war came to an end.

The logo of the new airline which was to become Zimbabwe's National Air Freight Carrier and which remained in operation until 2000 when it was wound up with substantial debts.
Source: http://en.wikipedia.org/wiki/File:Affretair_logo.jpg

Jack was now left with an airfreight company for which the timing was most fortuitous. Sanctions began to bite and having an air freight company which could operate jet aircraft from Salisbury via Libreville to Amsterdam was an asset to the Rhodesian Government. The return cargo was a variety of spares although Affretair took general cargo when it was available. At this time I was working in Johannesburg and arranged for Affretair to carry some large scale industrial air-conditioning equipment to Salisbury and then have it transported by road to South Africa. This assignment was conducted in an exemplary manner.

However it was still necessary to obtain from the Rhodesian Government the appropriate permits and licences and Air Rhodesia still had a lot of say in this matter. The need for a national air freight carrier may have become more apparent but Jack had to argue the case that he and not Air Rhodesia was the logical operator.

The argument was won by Jack who began to build up a large international network that functioned well and on most occasions delivered seamlessly. Because Affretair was ultimately owned by Rhodesia considerable care had to be given to avoiding any head-on confrontation with sanctions issues. Therefore Jack made it clear to everyone that he would not carry anything that could be considered militarily sensitive.

The first DC-8 had been acquired in 1972 but by 1975 Jack had acquired a second.

An article in the Rhodesian Herald which alludes to Jack's wide network of contacts.
Source: National Archives in Harare

One of Jack's DC-8s on route to the Air Trans Africa hangar.
Source:http://commons.wikimedia.org/wiki/File:Affretair_Douglas_DC-8_Marmet-3.jpg

Managing an airline is a most difficult business at a number of different levels ranging from technical issues, to administrative issues to strategy. Contributing materially to these difficulties is the fact that what an airline has for sale is a highly perishable commodity which has to be matched with an appropriate demand; the timing has to be exact and the price has to be just right for both the supplier and the purchaser. Jack was able to juggle all these issues at the same time which is not a skill easily imitated. He also built up around him a team of people who had bought into his vision of having a world class company which would eventually fly jet freighters around the world. It may be recalled that towards the end of the 1970s Affretair was carrying about 1,000 tons of produce a month out of Rhodesia. This cargo was going to a variety of countries in Africa and Europe. This was a major contributor to keeping the cogs of the Rhodesian economy turning.

By the way, back in April 1973 Air Rhodesia acquired 3 Boeing 720 jet liners and the country began to firmly move into the jet age. There is sometimes confusion about these aircraft. Although to the casual observer the Boeing 707 series of jets can be mistaken for DC-8s they are quite different and this deal for three 720s had nothing to do with Jack's airfreight business.

One of Air Rhodesia's Boeing 720s which was acquired shortly after Jack obtained his first DC-8 bringing a new lease of life to Air Rhodesia.
Source:*http://commons.wikimedia.org/wiki/File:Air_Rhodesia_Boeing_720_(6068614006).jpg?uselang=en-gb*

By 1980 it was decided that Affretair would become the property of the Rhodesian government as a separate entity which meant its future was secured. With Jack's death in 1982 Affretair's independence came into question and without Jack's leadership the company was taken over by Air Zimbabwe in 1983 while Air Zimbabwe was still a functioning entity. However by August 1997 it appears that one of Affretair's Douglas DC-8 Fs had been grounded as it no longer met required international safety standards. But by 1998 Affretair still appears to have been flying a Douglas DC-8F into Europe using Brussels as a hub. Eventually Affretair was liquidated in 2000 due to an enormous debt it had run up.

Decorations and Honors

By the end of the 1970s Jack had become a well known and highly admired citizen of Rhodesia. He was the owner of a substantial airline. He had made a recognizable contribution to circumventing aspects of the sanctions imposed on the country. He had also played a role by offering air transport support to the troops employed in

Fireforce in the Bush War. His contribution to the country was now beginning to be recognized in a number of ways.

A photograph of Jack's medals.
Source: Private collection of Greg and Ross Malloch

Jack received a number of honours and decorations and thus had a substantial collection of medals. The two which he regarded as most important were the CLM and the Air Force Medal. Jack received the Commander of the Legion of Merit (CLM) medal on November 11, 1978 from Ian Smith. He was also the last recipient of the Rhodesian Air Force's Independence Commemorative Decoration which he also received in 1978.

The Royal Aeronautical Society together with Rolls Royce initiated an award in Jack's name i.e. the Jack Malloch Trophy. This was to encourage newcomers to air transport engineering.

Also, what I think would have pleased him greatly, although he would not have admitted to it, Affretair named one of the DC-8s " Captain Jack Malloch".

Jack had accumulated some degree of wealth although this has been exaggerated. Most of this wealth was invested in his life work which was Affretair which of course enabled him to engage in projects such as the restoration of the spitfire.

And the Spitfire

Jack Malloch was a man who loved a challenge and with Affretair running comparatively routinely Jack's imagination turned to thinking about recapturing a piece of his past. His fighter pilot days had been of such importance to him and the spitfire at New Sarum reminded him of this period of his life.

In 1978 Jack requested and obtained permission to access the old spitfire airframe which had been displayed at New Sarum Air Force Station near Salisbury since 1954. It is not clear whether Jack formally obtained the ownership of this air force asset. This plane was restored by Jack and his colleagues with substantial help from the Rhodesian and South African Air Forces. The cost of restoring this air craft is not known but it has been estimated to have been at least a half million US dollars, a material amount of which would have been represented by the contribution made by the Affretair engineers over the two and a half years of painstaking work required. It is interesting to note that Jack was able to afford this type of investment in what was after all a non-commercial activity, some might even say a hobby. It appears that not everyone in Affretair was entirely positive about the spitfire as some saw this project as a distraction from the principal business of the company and a drain on their resources.

The old derelict Spitfire Mk22 on a plinth outside New Sarum Air Force base was to become a major project in Jack's life.
Source: Private collection of Nick Meikle.

The spitfire flew again in April 1980 and performed excellently. It was clearly Jack's pride and joy. Being in the cockpit of the Spitfire brought back a degree of freedom in the air which was one of his motivators in being a flyer in the first place, all those years ago.

It was a technological triumph to be able to restore this plane so completely and it made Jack into a minor international celebrity. This restoration work has been described as a miracle and I suppose the fact that it was conducted in the middle of Africa largely against the background of sanctions makes it a most remarkable event.

Jack inspecting the Spitfire.

Source: Private collection

It was certainly a feather in the cap for Rhodesian expertise and ingenuity and attracted international interest with a film being produced called *The Pursuit of a Dream*. The restored spitfire was now said to have been valued at one million US dollars. This was now the ultimate *"toy for a boy"*!

On March 26, 1982 Jack was demonstrating the capabilities of this wonderfully restored machine for the film crew who were making *Pursuit of a Dream*. The weather conditions were initially ideal but as can easily happen in Africa they rapidly changed.

Jack at the controls of his restored Spitfire. This was a very proud moment for everyone involved with the project.

Source: Private collection

The story I was told was that Jack was advised by the control tower at Harare Airport that a big black storm cloud was moving in on the area in which he was flying and that he should take evasive action. This is of course reminiscent of my experience with Jack in Francistown in 1966. However on this occasion Jack ignored the advice of the control tower and flew directly into the cloud.........where angels fear to tread.

The wreckage was found the following day in a remote area called Goromonzi. A local tribesman had walked three hours to the Juru Police station to report the crash.

The text below was posted on the War Bird Information Xchange website by PeterA [sic].

> "I was in charge of the 'Recovery Team' that was sent out from New Sarum Air Base to retrieve the wreckage - I say 'recovery' as there wasn't much to bring back. Unfortunately, I

wasn't involved in the navigation to the site, but as I remember it was about 160 [sic] kilometers North North East of Harare in a remote Tribal area.

The impact point was a large crater, with a debris field spreading out from there. The furtherest [sic] piece of wreckage was found about 400 metres from the crater - a 2 foot piece of laminated main spar. We were asked by the Board of Inquiry to locate the guns to give an acurate [sic] angle of attack, but after much fruitless digging in the soft, wet ground, the Board told us to stop. The evidence around the crater suggested a nose-down angle of about 16 degrees, with wings level and engine under power.

When the Board released the wreckage, they instructed us to collect everything, throw it into the crater and fill it in, which was done, except that the engine was loaded onto the recovery vehicle for further investigation later. The engine was a V8 as the front 4 cylinders had gone AWOL.... I seem to remember that someone rescued the tail wheel and arm as it was basically intact. Personally, I came away with a bent sodium-filled cylinder valve and the data plates from a Prop blade(German built) and the HX2 Generator. Apart from the undercarriage legs, the largest piece of wreckage was a 4 foot section of main spar."

There was no attempt at a forensic reconstruction of the aircraft or a formal inquest into Jack's death.

A memorial ceremony attended by a very large number of people was held at Warren Hills crematorium and Jack's ashes were left at that cemetery together with an appropriate plaque.

Jack was finally fully honoured by his country. Jack had come a long way from truck driver, to fighter pilot; from carrying a few hundred kilos of fresh fish from the coast to heading up an international air freight organisation transporting about 1,000 tons of fresh produce a month to Africa and Europe in direct defiance of the United Nations and others.

Unfortunately that cemetery in Harare has since been vandalised.

And the Fat Lady Sang

I met with Bob Nisbet shortly after Jack's death. The crash had demoralized everyone in Affretair. The shock was palpable and the atmosphere was grim. Jack was not a remote figurehead but was the one person to whom everyone in the organisation would have related. The Spitfire project had consumed company resources and time which some people in Affretair resented. Now it had taken Jack himself. As for Bob, he had spent his life in Jack's service. He had actually built his career on holding on to Jack's coat tails which were no more. At least he was not far from retirement and was looking forward to getting out of the company and was beginning to talk about a move south. Affretair in the early 1980s had become a corporate entity which was run largely by professional management. The fun had gone out of it for Bob who said that Jack had also found heading up this organisation which required such routine procedures increasingly dull.

There were other reasons why Affretair began to unravel. Deep in the DNA of the organisation was an ethos of supporting Rhodesia. The team that became Affretair had a greater objective than just running a commercial entity. Part of the glue that kept Affretair together was a belief in the Republic of Rhodesia and that in some sense they could successfully come out of the war. Although the idea of winning the war had been given up, Rhodesia was never defeated in the field. Affretair had been perceived as an important element, if not a crucial one, in keeping the rebel state going. The ideas that underpinned Rhodesia were now dead and had been buried at Lancaster House.

It is too simplistic to say that Jack was Affretair and Affretair was Jack as the organisation could not have functioned without the excellent team he had brought together. But Jack was much more than a corporate director. He was the embodiment of the ethos that kept the organisation running. When Affretair was brought under the wing of Air Zimbabwe, it was for many people time to move on. A number of the key members of the team dispersed and moved all over the world.

In any event it is unlikely that the complex business which Affretair had become could have lasted very long without Jack at the helm. He had fashioned Affretair in such a way that it would be nigh impossible for anyone else to fill his shoes.

A sad tale from Africa

As I wrote this account of Jack Malloch and his times I came to realise just how sad this period of history was in Africa. But then it occurred to me that Empires do not end well. The Spanish Empire disintegrated after wars in South and Central America in the early part of the 19th century. The Portuguese had a long period of bloody conflict in Brazil during this period.

The empires of Germany and Austria-Hungary only came to an end after the Great War – the war that was so awful that it was said to be the war that would end all wars. In the immediate aftermath of the demise of the Russian Empire i.e. in the years leading up to the creation of the Soviet Union it is said that nearly as many people were killed in the power struggles as were killed in the Great War itself. The collapse of the Ottoman Empire brought chaos to that region of the world with the loss on millions of lives, especially in Armenia.

One might take the view that the demise of the French and British Empires occurred relatively peacefully unless one is Vietnamese or Algerian or Kenyan and lost loved ones in these struggles.

Then the Biafran war may be seen as an attempt by some Nigerians to sort out the problems they inherited from the British Empire. They failed in this objective and Nigeria remains troubled to this day.

Rhodesia was in many ways a similar story involving an unsatisfactory withdrawal of Empire and a clumsy attempt to keep the old values of the imperial order alive.

On a personal level Jack's life might be considered sad because it was so much a struggle to establish an airline against very great odds. The attitude of Air Rhodesia and the Rhodesian Government in the early days would now be considered anticompetitive and completely unfair. The aircraft Jack had available to establish his charter service to Europe in the early 1960s let him down and almost destroyed his business. He needed to fly into risky places to rescue his near bankrupt business and take chances which were beyond what he naturally wanted to do. As a result he spent time in detention in the most dreadful circumstances on the equator. He built up the airline to find that he really needed Government backing to make it work the way it had to and in so doing lost control of his business. He then found himself drawn into the Bush War at home. Finally his airline was nationalised.

In the last years of his life Jack found a project which brought him considerable pride and joy which is clearly evidenced by his attitude captured on video on the day the spitfire first flew after restoration.

Sadly the Spitfire was also the instrument of this death.

Looking back from the 21st century

There are of course two stories told in this book. There is the story of Air Trans Africa which is nothing more or less than the story of Jack Malloch and there is the story of the loss of empire in Rhodesia. These two stories are intrinsically interrelated and the former cannot be told without the latter.

Looking back at Air Trans Africa and Jack Malloch I am surprised by a number of things. First of all the code of silence worked so well. And I was so interested in getting the job done that I was doing that I didn't try to ask more questions and get some answers. I am sure that if I had asked carefully I would have learnt a lot more about what was going on.

I was always curious about how the air crews lived without their salaries being paid. I had known about the trouble in Katanga and of course I knew about MoïseTshombe. It only occurred to me later that at least some if not most of the air crew had made bags of money out of that war and they could easily live on the few pounds a month Jack had been paying them when I arrived at Air Trans Africa. They were waiting for the next lucrative war.

It never occurred to me to ask about Jack's international network. I went to Paris with him once and I didn't think of asking anything about the men in suits we met there. They were a very POSH highly cultivated group of functionaries. But who or what was the ultimate paymaster? It is probably not very difficult to guess. But Jack's network was much bigger than just the French connection. How did it happen that Jack was able to acquire the original DC-4, the Super Connie and the Dove? There is a story in that as well.

I wonder about some of the crew. For example it occurred to me that the elderly Chief Pilot might not have passed his medical elsewhere. Were all the crew properly rated for the aircraft they flew?

The components in the store room which were picked up in various places in the world were probably from abandoned aircraft. Were they really good enough? However I flew quite happily on the Super Connie and the first DC-7F Jack bought.

The people who were critical of Jack saw him as a maverick and in some senses he was and it is true that in aviation being a maverick can be dangerous. But I think that Jack was a maverick because of force of circumstances. Would he have been just as content running a normal airline if the National Carrier had been more flexible and there were no sanctions and a Bush War to contend with? It is hard to answer such a question.

The spitfire episode shines another light on Jack. The resources required to restore that aircraft were enormous and one wonders if in a war-torn Rhodesia they were employed most efficaciously in the pursuit of Jack's dream. In viewing the photograph of Jack climbing into the spitfire cockpit I have to ask myself whether a man of 62 years old should really be flying an aircraft which was such an effective tool when used by 20 year olds some 40 years before. In addition that photograph caused me to recall a comment made by Jack in a newspaper interview a few years before to the effect that he would continue to fly as long as the medical officers continued to certify him as fit to do so. This love of flying can result in men flying beyond the time in life when they should really have stopped.

I also wonder about the big black cloud. In 1966 Jack wanted to get out of Francistown as quickly as possible to avoid the oncoming weather front. In 1982 he decided to fly into one. The pilot in the accompanying Vampire commented on just how formidable this really was and Jack clearly should have avoided it.

I worked for Jack because I had an interesting job of work to do. I was learning on the job, doing work I had not done before. Other employers would have sought someone with much more experience than me. In working for Jack Malloch there was a sense of adventure. I was paid well enough. I had a share of a pretty horrible office but so then did everyone else. And I also fell for the corporate dream that I was contributing to the important international airline that Jack was building. I have puzzled over how it was that Jack was able to sell this dream to so many people around me and I don't have a satisfactory answer to this question. It is something to do with what Iris Nesbit had said about Jack's peculiar leadership abilities. Somehow Jack had the knack of making people feel that they were very special and that they were especially close to him. This is a gift which only quite special leaders have.

Jack is clearly remembered fondly by his many friends. His contribution to aviation in Africa is without doubt quite unique.

Looking back on the story of the Rhodesian bid for independence and the war that followed there are many different questions to ask. Did the British renege on their promise to allow Southern Rhodesia to become independent on their own terms? Was there really a special understanding if not an actual promise of this happening? Should politicians not expect circumstances to change and promises to be broken?

Could Rhodesia have won the Bush War? Can any established regime defeat a popular insurgency? What would it mean to say that the incumbent regime had won such a war if there was still an unsatisfied population? It is now understood in a way that it was not in the 1960s and 1970s that wars need politically orientated end games and this is especially true with respect to war involving insurgents. This is of course problematic because it can be difficult to know with whom the government forces should actually negotiate and it is often emotionally difficult to talk to people who are about to become the former enemy. For much of the Bush War Smith's end game was that the Rhodesian military would destroy the guerrillas. In talking to veterans it is interesting to hear some of them say that they thought that they could win the war even towards the end of the 1970s. However an objective assessment of the possibility of this would have led to the realisation that there was a virtually endless supply of people backed by the Soviet Union and China who were prepared to fight for the termination of white rule in Rhodesia. The war had been all but lost by the time Smith realised that a political settlement was going to be necessary and what he set up in conjunction with Bishop Muzorewa was too little too late.

Harold Wilson did not bring the Smith government down in months but in the end others defeated Smith for him and thus he did not have to pay much of the cost of the war in either treasure or lives. The Beira Patrol which actually saw no action to speak of was the only military involvement by Great Britain. It may have taken a long time to resolve but the Rhodesia situation ended up as the mother country wanted. And Wilson received little or no credit for being smart enough to keep his country out of an African War. He was also brave enough to resist the pressure he was put under to join the Americans in Vietnam.

It is also interesting to ask what the French were doing in their support for Rhodesia. Affretair played a significant role in sustaining the Rhodesian society by delivering goods along the Amsterdam Libreville Salisbury route. This could not have been done without the approval of the French Government. Thus in the same way as French support had kept the Biafran war going, French support may be said to have prolonged the Bush War. What was in it for France? Did the French Republic with its belief in *Liberté, Egalité, Fraternité* actually favour the continuance of white rule in Africa? It has been said by some that they were primarily mischief making for their old adversaries, *Perfidious Albion*. On the other hand French industry did well out of the Rhodesian market which had been abandoned by the British.

Ian Smith probably could have avoided the war or at least retained white control for longer without having to declare independence. Smith could have agreed to Wilson's demands and then systematically undermined all these demands in practice. No doubt such a strategy would have caught up with Rhodesia in the end but the white minority government might have been able to buy another 10 or even 20 years with appropriate delaying tactics. It was often said that Ian Smith was too honest to be a politician. Would a peaceful transference of power in 1965 or 1966 have led to a different Zimbabwe to the one we have today? The answer to this is almost certainly yes but would it have been a better country? Better for whom is a key aspect of this question?

In the end I am reminded of how difficult it is to kick the habit of the Empire. It is probably true to say that no Empire ever gave up without a struggle which was costly in terms of both life and treasure. FW De Klerk's comment about why the Nationalist Party in South Africa abandoned apartheid seems to be relatively enlightened. Of course, apartheid had already cost quite a few lives and a pile of money when De Klerk began to negotiate with Mandela. All that can be added is that FW De Klerk's understanding of the situation was indubitably fashioned by the experiences of Ian Smith and his struggle to avoid majority rule. Perhaps to reach his enlightened view President De Klerk needed to have witnessed Smith's failed attempt to stem the retreating tide of white imperialism in much the same way as King Canute failed to stop the tide coming in with his royal commands. The age of the white man's political domination in Africa was over and this was not going to be changed. Whether the new regimes which would replace the old white ones would be better or worse was simply not an issue worthy of any consideration.

Index

Afro-Continental Airways, 74
Air Rhodesia, 3, 8, 14, 17, 33, 34, 75, 83, 87, 94- 96, 105
Alamo, 90, 92
Anglo-Boer War, 38, 90
Angola, 45, 54, 88, 91
Atlantic Charter, 42, 44
Auxiliary Air Force, 2
Beira Patrol, 51, 52, 109
Belgian Congo, 40
Biafra, vii, 57, 58, 59, 61, 63, 64, 65, 66, 67, 68, 71, 72, 74, 92, 93
Black soldiers, 35
Blantyre, 15, 16, 21
Boeing 707, 18, 95
British Commonwealth, 46
BSAP, 26, 72
Burma, 36
Bush War, ii, 79, 80, 85- 90, 97, 105-110
Carnation Revolution, 84
Central African Federation, 47
Chief Flight Engineer, 22
Chief Pilot, 22, 107
Chimurenga, 80
China, 80, 81, 82, 90, 109
Cold War, 59, 81
DC-4, 60, 66, 107
DC-7C, 8, 19, 64
DC-7F, 64, 65, 107
DC-8, iv, 18, 79, 94, 95, 96, 98
Decorations, vii, 96
Fireforce, 85, 97
Fish Air, 2, 24
Francistown, 14, 101, 108
FRELIMO, 82, 84
Gabon, 58, 63, 74, 92, 93
Harold Wilson, 48, 49, 52, 81, 109
Hausa, 55, 56
Igbo, 55, 56, 57
Johannesburg, 27, 93
Kissinger, vii, 88, 89, 90, 91
Lockheed Super Constellation, 8, 18, 20
Lomé, 69, 70, 71
MacMillan, 36, 37, 38
MAF, 21
Malawi, 15, 16, 21, 27, 48, 54
Mau Mau, 41
Mother country, 52, 53
Mugabe, 80, 92
Muzorewa, 88, 109
Nigerian civil war, 54
Nkomo, 80, 92
Nyasaland, 2, 47, 48
ORAFS, v
Port Harcourt, 62
Rhodesian Air Services, 2
Rhodesian Front, 48, 53, 76
Royal Navy, 51
Salazar, 82, 83, 84
Sanctions, 52, 93
South Africa, v, 1, 14, 18, 26, 29, 34- 37, 44-46, 51- 54, 62, 75, 76, 81-93, 98, 110
Soviet Union, 58, 80, 81, 82, 90, 104, 109
Spitfire, vii, 98, 99, 100, 101, 103, 106
Steptoe and Son, 79
Super Connie, 8, 9, 66, 74, 107
Swiss Bank, 12
Switzerland, 60, 67, 68, 69
Uli, 62, 65
UN Resolution, 53
VC 10, 28
Viscount, 14, 83, 87
Vorster, 88
Windhoek, 20, 74, 75
Woodrow Wilson, 42
Yoruba, 55, 56

www.ingramcontent.com/pod-product-compliance
Ingram Content Group UK Ltd.
Pitfield, Milton Keynes, MK11 3LW, UK
UKHW021253180426
11947UKWH00010B/756